THE VERDICT

ACHIEVING AN OPTIMAL WORK-LIFE BALANCE

Robert Cuomo Ph.D.

John DiCicco Ph.D.

ISBN: 979-8-218-42239-4

Dedications

The irony of human existence is that the stronger and brighter fall prey to life-sapping illnesses. The two most common are dementia and Parkinson's disease. So it was with my father, Crimens Pacy (1908 to 1995). He was a physically powerful man who honed his stamina and strength from an early age as a laborer and farmer. With only a 6th-grade education, he built a remarkably successful farming business. He lived to be 87. Spending his last two years in a nursing home, he was a strong man until near the end, when Parkinson's took command of him. His will and strength gave us all hope and comfort that we could overcome limits. His efforts teach us that we acquire the strength we need to overcome.

–Ron Pacy

This book is dedicated to Sandra Pacy, a dear friend for many years who had faced Parkinson's Disease with dignity and determination. Her zest for living life to its fullest and her compassion for others benchmarked her decision to face any obstacle, big or small, head-on and never look back. Sandy passed away peacefully on April 7th, 2024, holding her husband Ron Pacy's hand after completing fifty-six beautiful years of marriage.

–John DiCicco

My father, Pasquale Cuomo, was afflicted with Parkinson's Disease at the early age of forty. He was the victim of early-onset Parkinson's and lived with its effects on him for thirty years. I dedicate this book to his memory and to those who have experienced or will experience early-onset Parkinson's. May ongoing research lead to a cure for this affliction.

–Robert Cuomo, PH.D.

Table of Contents

Robert J. Cuomo

Dr. Robert J. Cuomo is President of *The Cuomo Consulting Group*, a firm which specializes in executive leadership, coaching, and helping individuals make effective career decisions. Dr. Cuomo is the former Dean of the Girard School of Business at Merrimack College in North Andover, MA and Founding Dean of the School of Business at Dean College in Franklin, MA. He earned a Ph. D. in Economics from Boston College in 1977 and graduated summa cum laude from Merrimack College. He has an extensive professional network, has held senior management positions in the corporate, consulting, and higher education industries, and understands effective organizational management and what it takes to be successful in today's rapidly changing business world. He has designed and implemented numerous programs to foster executive development, and has been instrumental in building bridges between the academic and business worlds.

Robert J. Cuomo is the Chief Financial Officer of *The Joey Fournier Services*, a 501(c3) organization. The organization provides after-school activities in Lawrence, MA Public Schools. The program focuses on activities that reinforce violence prevention and prosocial skills such as empathy, impulse control, anger management, problem-solving, and conflict resolution.

Dr. Cuomo has provided expert witness testimony before legislative bodies, including the U.S Congress and the Massachusetts Department of Public Utilities. He is frequently interviewed by newspapers and radio stations to provide commentary on leadership and economic issues. He has written columns for the *Eagle Tribune*, appeared regularly on WCAP radio, and has been a frequent guest on the local cable television station.

Dr. Cuomo has taught economics courses at Boston College, Babson College, Merrimack College, Dean College, Lasell University, Cambridge College and the University of Phoenix. These courses have included Industrial Organization, Public Finance, Econometrics, International Trade, Labor Economics, Economic Development, Comparative Economic Systems, Business Ethics and Negotiations.

On a personal note, Dr. Cuomo lives in North Andover and has been married to his wife Donna for 53 years. They have two adult children, Mark and Rachel, both of whom live locally.

John A. DiCicco

Dr. DiCicco taught in the Business Department at Curry College in Milton, MA from 1999-2021. He taught several business- and business-related courses with a specialization in leadership. Since, 2019, Professor DiCicco has been a senior affiliate faculty member at Wentworth Institute of Technology in the School of Management, specializing in communications, project management, marketing, organizational behavior, and leadership.

Dr. DiCicco served as the Campus College Chair of Graduate Business Management Programs at the University of Phoenix, Massachusetts Campuses, from 2007-2014. Between 2014-2016, he also taught Micro and Macro Economics at Dean College in Franklin, MA.

From 1991 to present, Dr. DiCicco has served as the president of Organizational Analysis Systems, a management consulting group located in Brockton, MA, specializing in organizational and leadership consulting and training to upper and middle level managers, in order to be more responsible leaders in their respective fields.

DiCicco has authored or coauthored *Leadership is a Choice*, *The Leadership Gene*, and *The Authentic Leader*. Leadership podcasts and newsletters can be found on theauthenticleadercd.com. He can be contacted at johnoasi@comcast.net.

Dr. DiCicco earned his Ph.D. in Higher Education Administration and Professional Development at Capella University in Minneapolis, MN in 2001. He has been happily married to his wife of 43 years, Gale, and has an adult son Eric. All reside in Brockton, MA.

Foreword

By Jordan Rich
WBZ Radio Boston, iHeart Media

The Verdict completes a provocative trilogy, a dramatic arc of living, breathing characters, fictional beings with recognizable hopes, dreams, fears, and setbacks. We continue to see a lot of ourselves in these characters, which explains why the books and accompanying workshops/seminars are so very impactful.

Readers of the previous two books in *The Authentic Leader* series have come to know much about the public and private lives of Josh and Lynn, and their daughter Jessica. Their professional lives have often been successful, but not always. How they deal with crises in the workplace, while attempting to retain balance in the family, presents an ideal setting for situational questions of leadership. But not merely questions; the books offer valuable lessons and guidance on how to not only survive, but thrive.

The choice of the title in this latest installment is an apt one. A verdict implies a trial has been adjudicated. The characters in this story are undergoing stressful trials, some of them acute and life-threatening. The family is living through an abundance of dramatic, life-altering events. The story is cleverly constructed to offer scenarios that will make us think, react, critique, and empathize through introspection and lessons learned.

None of us escapes unscathed from this life. People are challenged every day by unexpected roadblocks and dangers. As the old expression goes, "Man plans, and God laughs!" Life has a way of shaking us of course, often in the blink of an eye.

The Verdict focuses on how characters learn to adapt, making their share of mistakes along the way. There are hard lessons to be learned, and rarely any quick or easy solutions. Beset with misfortune, Josh and Lynn are forced to make major changes and sharp decisions. Through their actions, our authors raise key questions about how any of us deal with our own set of challenges. Helpful guidance on leading a better life is a key part of the process here, with lessons derived from ethical principles as old as time itself, and faith in the resilience of the human spirit.

There is drama on every page. But also hope and understanding.

This book provides the impetus for us to think about struggle. How we respond to tough circumstances significantly determines our path forward. This is the verdict ultimately for all of us.

I am personally inspired and challenged by the stories and leadership lessons in John's and Bob's book *The Verdict*. The exact book I want my students to read to learn about leadership.

Mohammad M. Agwa, MBA, Ph.D.
Associate Professor
Fisher College, Boston, MA

Life challenge; stress-related conflict (disagreements between Josh and Lynn); discovery (what one learns about oneself and how it relates to others); resolution of where we go from here (resolve to keep going better than before); execution of a plan.

It is a compelling story about two highly successful professional people navigating severe life challenges, while trying to maintain their enormous responsibilities. It is a well-written story about the journey through life's challenges.

Ralph Longo
ERP Business Systems Administrator

I love how easy this is to read vs. the arduousness of typical leadership books. The characters are endearing and right from the start, left me wanting to read more. In particular, my favorite parts of the book are the summaries at the end of each chapter. Providing thought-provoking questions and lessons in bite-size pieces is such a great way to get readers to digest the principles. Thanks for sharing your work!

Maryanne Basler, CPC, CX-II
Senior Manager, Customer Success - Payer
(she/her/hers)

In their book *The Verdict*, Dr. Cuomo and Dr. DiCicco bring together clear examples of the relevance of an intense academic experience combined with the practicality of real world corporate contention. The book provides an excellent resource for corporate and academic leadership programs. It is an essential read for all those interested in career development and enhancement.

Richard J. Santagati
Senior Executive capacities for publicly-traded and privately-owned organizations, and higher educational institutes

The Verdict is the last and, probably, the most important book of the trilogy that includes two earlier books by Dr. Robert Cuomo and Dr. John DiCicco - *The Authentic Leader* and *Differencia*. It is dedicated to defining leadership skills and helping readers to develop their potential as effective and compassionate leaders. When we hear the word "leader" we think of prominent political and military figures and CEOs of big corporations. Most of us don't apply the notion of leadership to ourselves and people around us. In this trilogy, the authors set out to show how ordinary people deal with difficult situations in their personal and professional lives. Throughout the entire trilogy, the fictional characters – Joshua Keating, Lynn Ann Marconi and their now 9-year-old daughter are facing challenging issues. They are required to make important decisions involving their relationships, family and the company where both Josh and Lynn work. While a plot based on a family and professional conflicts is a given for good fiction, *The Verdict,* as well as its predecessors, is much more than just entertainment. Its format – a chapter in which the plot is developed, followed by the recap of issues and then questions to ponder – is the most valuable concept, allowing the reader to identify and develop important leadership skills.

It is my opinion that each person is required to be a leader at some point in their life – be it in the work environment, in relationships, or in many life situations. I also think that without training, most of us, humans, tend to freeze in difficult situations. However, some are able to pull themselves together and lead the rest through. It is not necessarily a talent, but rather a set of life circumstances in the past that prepared them to take on the leadership role in an isolated case. *The Verdict* with its Questions to Ponder is ultimately an important tool which could be used by individuals in honing their leadership skills and by organizational leaders or professionals in helping to develop leadership skills and initiative in employees.

Elizabeth Sinoff

Retired Economist and Real Estate Business owner

In a captivating way, *The Verdict* builds upon the authors' previous books, *The Authentic Leader* and *Differencia*, to illustrate that truly successful, sustainable leadership is simply not possible without authenticity. With relatable scenarios and thought-provoking questions, *The Verdict* enables readers to handle the myriad leadership challenges they encounter with confidence and effectiveness. This is a must-read for people at all stages of their careers.

Roseanne Thomas

Founder and President of Protocol Advisors, Inc.
Boston, MA

In *The Verdict,* Dr. Cuomo and Dr. DiCicco have provided the capstone to the corporate journey that they started in *The Authentic Leader* and continued in *Differencia.* The fast-paced culmination to the trilogy draws the reader in from the very first page, to a complicated integration of personal, life-changing scenarios intertwined with business and corporate decision-making events. Each chapter is organized to analyze these steadily complicating but realistic personal situations that also impact the major business issues and decisions of Differencia! Each challenge identifies the tools required, analytical paradigms needed, as well as thoughtful discussion points for solving the intertwined relationship between personal and business solutions. These result in clear opportunities to demonstrate leadership in both personal and corporate situations, which, as it turns out, may not actually be that different! The ambitious effort to link considerations of personal, life-altering struggles with major corporate direction decisions, while also indicating how sound management theory can be applied to both with positive results… works! A unique and useful approach, as well as a fascinating and entertaining read! I loved this book!

Jeanne M. Colachico, Esquire
Jeanne M. Colachico, Esquire & Associates
North Andover, MA

Introduction

The future holds many uncertainties for Josh, Lynn, and Jessica. The union of this family is facing many challenges yet to be seen and many obstacles to overcome physically, emotionally, and spiritually. However, one thing is for sure. They love each other unconditionally. This much has been proven, as the last two books, *The Authentic Leader* and *Differencia*, have shown.

The book you are about to read, *The Verdict*, will further the self-discovery of the three main characters in this progressive narrative of inner contemplation and reflection on what authentic leadership means, and why it is so challenging to create a culture for successful decision-making.

I ask the readers to put themselves in the "driver's seat" of the main characters and envision their actions as yours. What would you do under the circumstances? What would you recommend? I highly recommend reading the first two books in the series before you read this one. After you've made your preliminary recommendations, I recommend reading and answering the questions in this book's "Lessons Learned" section.

Happy Reading!

John

Chapter 1
The Verdict

It is Monday, October 3, 2022, at 9:00 AM. I am walking hand in hand with Lynn to Dr. Pereira's office for a 10:00 AM appointment to discuss Lynn's prognosis, and perhaps our collective professional futures at Differencia. I can smell the burnt aroma of the old wood grain on the hardwood floors of ancient shipbuilding from the late 1800s, built over 150 years ago that was converted into doctors' offices a decade ago. Dr. Pereira's office is the fourth office on the left as we enter the third floor of the building.

We arrive in the waiting area, and all is well up to this point. I walk over to the coat rack and hang up my blazer, only to find Lynn missing from where we were standing a minute ago, waiting to sit down and waiting for the doctor to call us to discuss her prognosis.

I begin to panic and wonder what just happened at the last minute. I am looking everywhere, and there is no trace of Lynn. My first reaction is to call her on her cell phone, but that isn't going to happen because her cell phone is lying on top of her coat under the seat she would be sitting on, when I returned to get her coat to hang up on the rack next to mine.

It is now approaching 9:45 AM, and there is no trace of Lynn anywhere. I begin to perspire and have no clue where to look. I ask one of the female attendants to check the ladies' rooms and see if

Lynn has gone into one of them without telling me. The attendants did not find Lynn in any of the ladies' rooms. What am I going to do now? Where do I go to look for Lynn?

I leave the waiting area and take the elevator to the second floor, and there is no sign of Lynn. I proceed to the first floor, and Lynn is still waiting to be seen. At this moment, I feel so alone and so scared that I am crying as if I was a two-year-old toddler who just got his rattle taken from him. I am a company CEO with eleven thousand employees, acting foolishly and selfishly. I am embarrassed. I should be thinking of Lynn and not me. I need to focus. It is now 10:05 AM. We are late for our appointment, and Lynn is nowhere to be found. I need to focus.

I am realizing that my emotions cannot take me over ever again. I need to think coherently and strategically and accept the outcome of what just happened as what it is rather than what I want it to be. In short, I need to grow up! OK, Josh, get your act together and look for Lynn. I should call Dr. Pereira, as I am sure he is wondering where Lynn is now. I make the call and go into Dr. Pereira's answering service. I don't panic and leave a message about what is happening now. I will wait for his response.

In the interim, while waiting for Dr. Pereira to call me back, I migrate out the front door of the old shipbuilding, and my eyes are drawn across the street. I see Lynn at the bus stop sitting under the shelter of a waiting bench where people go to wait for the bus to arrive. I am horrified, and my heart is breaking simultaneously with what my senses are taking in. I am still trying to figure out where to begin or what to do now.

I hold my composure and walk across the street to the bus stop waiting area to see if Lynn recognizes me. This could be better. Every muscle in my body is tightening, and I am afraid to open my mouth. I slowly approach Lynn, gently sit beside her, and grab her hand. She needs me right now, and nothing else matters to me. I never realized how much I love this woman and understand that this moment is the verdict of every choice we make about ourselves and our future. I now realize that I was wrong. Lynn's prognosis of her future with Differencia does not drive us to succeed. What drives us to be successful in life is making ourselves the best version of ourselves for better or worse. We will survive, two as one.

The driver of this narrative will continue to unfold *The Verdict* just discovered. The rest is up to you, the reader, to take this journey with Lynn and me as the narrative unfolds chapter by chapter in this book.

Lessons Learned

Lynn walks with Josh to an appointment in Dr. Pereira's office.

Lynn disappears as Josh hangs up his blazer on the coat rack in Dr. Pereira's office.

Josh begins to panic when he cannot locate Lynn.

Josh wonders where he should look for Lynn.

Josh chastises himself for feeling sorry for himself instead of focusing on Lynn.

Josh calls Dr. Pereira to inform him of Lynn's leaving the hospital grounds.

Josh walks across the street and sees Lynn at the bus stop sitting under the shelter of a waiting bench. He concentrates on Lynn's condition and muses that they can work together to survive personally and professionally.

Questions to Ponder

Is Josh's reaction to Lynn's absence rational?

If not, how should he have acted?

Have you ever faced a similar emergency in your life?

What did you learn from the consequences of Josh's reaction?

Is Josh's self-flagellation of Lynn's leaving the hospital healthy?

Does it facilitate effective decision-making?

Have you reacted this way in a similar circumstance?

How can you reduce the temptation to self-admonish?

Key Leadership Qualities Identified

Introspection - Examine one's mental and emotional process, analyzes the consequences of one's behavior on goal attainment, and deduces a better course of action.

Patience - Not expecting immediate results. Quite often, the impact of a decision works with LAG. Ignoring this practice works against goal attainment.

Socratic Questioning - Asking open-ended questions. Allowing others to explain their thoughts. It leads to a better understanding of others and establishing strong relationships.

Positive Thinking - It combats the tendency to "catastrophize" possible outcomes. It focuses on favorable outcomes resulting from a decision. Optimistic individuals tend to have an entrepreneurial mindset, which leads to business success.

Contingency Planning - Considering all possible outcomes from a decision. Effective leaders are always prepared to change a course of action if a change of circumstances occurs. "The future belongs to those who prepare for it."

Situational Awareness - Being conscious of the environment in which one is operating. Successful leaders conduct PESTEL analysis. They recognize the environment's political, economic, social, technological, environmental, and legal aspects.

Chapter 2
Where Do We Go From Here?

Life has no guarantees, yet it often is full of challenges and surprises. Sometimes we are prepared for them. Sometimes we are not. However, one thing is for sure. They will happen without our permission. In my world, this is yet another challenge and surprise. Although I have had several of them before, this one will decide our collective fates. This, I am sure!

I take a deep breath. I gently grab Lynn's other hand and softly ask, "Are you OK?" Lynn's eyes meet mine. Her hands began to perspire, and her mouth trembling trying to get the words out to me. I respond. "It's OK, baby. Take your time. I am not going anywhere." Finally, Lynn shouts out to me in a loud voice. "Josh, why am I sitting here across the street from where we were supposed to have our appointment? Did we have the appointment already? I don't remember anything!"

In my mind it is obvious what just happened. Lynn had another memory lapse and a major one. This happened when she was ready to have her appointment with Dr. Pereira. This is quite a coincidence. There was also a reason for everything. I gently hold onto both of Lynn's hands and ask her to take a deep breath and rest for a minute. As I explain to Lynn what has transpired in the last half hour, Dr. Pereira returns my call. I ask Lynn to continue to rest while waiting for the bus where she was sitting and tell her I must answer a phone call relating to work. Lynn smiles at me as I excuse myself to take the call. I do not want her to know I am talking to Dr. Pereira.

"Hello, Dr. Pereira; this is Josh Keating. I'm truly sorry for the delay in getting to your office. My wife Lynn has had a setback, and I'm unsure what happened or why. We are sitting at the bus stop across the street, and I'm trying to figure out why Lynn left the building just before her appointment."

Dr. Pereira responds. "Josh, sometimes these things happen, and we can't explain why." I told Dr. Pereira I would do my best and let him know immediately. The doctor reminds me he has another appointment at 11:00 AM at the hospital, which he cannot break. I told him I would do my best to get Lynn to come to his office and keep him posted. If you can get Lynn to come to my office safely, I can assess the situation and decide whether this is an appropriate time to share her prognosis with both of you.

I return to the bus stop, and Lynn is still sitting on the bench in the waiting area. She remained calm as I explained what happened less than an hour ago. She tells me she can return to Dr. Pereira's office for our appointment. I tell her that we only have a window of approximately 30 minutes in our appointment today and may need to reschedule our time with him, under the circumstances. Lynn nods her head in agreement, and we make our way back to the office building across the street. We take the elevator to the third floor, and He is outside his office waiting for us.

Dr. Pereira smiles at us both and welcomes us into his office. He escorts us to comfortable leather seats with armrests, in front of his desk, and asks if we would like coffee or bottled water. Both Lynn and I decline and are very anxious to hear his report. However, before the doctor starts a conversation, he looks at Lynn directly in her eyes and asks, "What do you think just happened, Lynn?" I was startled that he would even ask that question under the circumstances. However, he sat patiently, waiting for an answer to his question.

Lynn responds. "I don't know, Dr. Pereira." The doctor follows her response. "To the best of your recollection, what is the last thing you remember when you arrived at my office?" Lynn appears reflective and relaxed as she tries to collect her thoughts on the morning's events. She responds. "I remember sitting in the waiting area of your office while Josh was sitting next to me. I checked my smartwatch, which illuminated the time as 9:39 AM. I remember Josh taking off his blazer jacket and getting up to hang it on the coat rack by the door near your office. That is the last thing that I remember, Dr. Pereira."

Dr. Pereira responds most intuitively. "Do you remember leaving this office building and walking over to the bus stop?" Lynn appears to be confused by the question and immediately gives a blank stare to the doctor. "Do you recall if you were looking for something you might have misplaced, after Josh got up to hang his blazer, which is the last thing you said you remembered?" She responds. "Dr. Pereira, I remember removing my blazer and putting it under my chair in the waiting room outside your office." He responds "Lynn, do you remember anything else you did after you put your coat under your seat?" She thinks pensively for a moment and says. "I remember looking at my cell phone and checking my messages." Lynn suddenly stops talking and stares blankly at Dr. Pereira, and then at me. She responds in horror "My God, I checked my messages, and a calendar reminder stated that my appointment with Dr. Pereira was scheduled in 20 minutes. That is the last thing I remember."

Dr. Pereira, upon hearing this, looks at her most inquisitively and responded "Lynn, do you remember putting your cell phone on your coat, under the seat in the waiting room?" Lynn looks at Dr. Pereira and shakes her head, no." He says "Josh, isn't this what you told me on the phone, earlier at the bus stop, and described that Lynn's cell phone was on top of her coat, under the seat in the waiting room where she was sitting?" I nodded affirmatively.

Dr. Pereira says "Lynn and Joshua, this confirms the prognosis of the report I am about to give you, about Lynn's condition after six months of being away from her job. I want you to absorb what I am about to tell you, and then leave here and process everything I tell you today, as my best advice."

He continues. "After six months of careful diagnosing and testing, all your blood work remains normal, except for high levels of Cortisol in your blood. The six months you took away from your job did not decrease them. Some dangers involved include impairment of learning and memory, mood swings, high blood pressure, weight gain, and bone density loss; in your case, memory impairment increases with increased stress levels."

Dr. Pereira takes off his glasses and looks at both of us. "It is my professional recommendation, as the top neurologist in a major hospital in Los Angeles, that you do not, Lynn, under the circumstances of your medical condition, return to Differencia as their CEO, in a full-time capacity. However, it is your choice. Today was a powerful but impactful example of what could happen to you on the job if your stress increases to dangerous levels, putting your health in serious jeopardy. Lynn, if you choose to work, you need to do something else, rather than remain the CEO of the company that employs 11,000 individuals. It is just too much, in my professional opinion."

Dr. Pereira continues. "I know this is painful to hear for both of you. However, as a physician with many years of experience as a neurologist, I watched everything you experienced medically, from when you got off the plane when returning to LA from Boston, to now. Josh, it would be best if you did the same thing. It would be best if you exercised your options. In the final analysis, the decision is yours. Whatever you decide, do what is best for both of you."

Our meeting ended just before 10:45 AM, and Dr. Pereira was already off to his next appointment. We will go home tonight and discuss where we will go from here with our professional and personal lives.

Lessons Learned

The current situation is a significant challenge for Josh and Lynn.

Lynn does not remember why she's at the bus stop, sitting on a bench, and wonders if she has missed an appointment.

Dr. Pereira returns Josh's call to discuss Lynn's medical prognosis.

Dr. Pereira tells Josh to schedule an appointment with him as soon as possible.

Josh and Lynn returned to Dr. Pereira's office to discuss Lynn's medical condition.

Dr. Pereira asks Lynn if she remembers what happened.

Lynn remembers sitting in Dr. Pereira's office and watching Josh hang up his blazer on the coat rack. She remembers that she has an appointment with Dr. Pereira in 20 minutes.

Dr. Pereira asks Lynn if she remembers putting her cell phone on a coat under the seat. Lynn says she does not remember that.

Dr. Pereira tells Lynn and Josh that after extensive tests, there is a significant risk of learning impairment, and he has added that physical impairment to her system could occur if she is confronted by stress. He tells her he recommends that she not return as CEO of Differencia.

Questions to Ponder

Is Dr. Pereira's presentation of Lynn's medical condition to her and Josh too harsh?

Should he have sugarcoated it in some way?

Do you tend to sugarcoat bad news, to soften the blow of potential outcomes?

If so, please provide some examples.

Do you agree with Dr. Pereira's recommendation that Lynn not return as CEO of Differencia for the time being? Why or why not?

Have you ever been faced with a transfer of responsibilities for a worker under your supervision, in order to mitigate the health impact of stress in their current position?

Key Leadership Qualities Identified

Empathy - Striving to understand the feelings and circumstances of others. In the words of Dale Carnegie, "put yourself in the other guy's shoes." To develop followers, leaders must understand the needs of others and develop a strategy to recruit them.

Vulnerability - Simply stated it is being totally transparent and trustworthy. Successful leaders "say what they mean and mean what they say." They do not equivocate. This leads to developing trust in themselves from others.

Trust - Leaders trust others in their daily interactions. They trust but verify. They take others at face value until they observe a negative behavior pattern.

Emotional Quotient - The ability to recognize the environment in which one operates. It ranks higher than technical skills in the attributes of authentic leaders and is essential to leadership success.

Teamwork - Working with others to achieve a goal or objective. In the sports world, winning is not necessarily achieved by the team with the most talent. Quite often, the team with more grit or determination wins. "Attitude, not aptitude, often determines altitude."

Character - Consistently acting to be true to one's values and principles It is what you do when no one is looking. It means not doing things just for show.

Successorship - Leaders develop others in their organization to continue to be successful when the leader is gone. This requires careful training and mentoring.

Chapter 3

Life is a Marathon, Not a Sprint

After receiving the news from Dr. Pereira, we drove in silence back to our townhouse, after I informed my senior staff that I would be at work sometime mid-afternoon, and phone or text me with anything urgent. For the most part, I have cleared my meeting schedule for today's appointment with the neurologist.

We drive into our parking garage at our townhouse. Still, Lynn has not said a word and is staring out the car window at the scenery. I look at her and smile as I shut off the engine of our SUV. I get out of the car, and Lynn remains in her seat with a blank stare, facing the scenery outside the garage. I am telling you all this because I want you to know I don't know what is coming next, as I speak to you in this narrative. I am wondering what she will say. I am considering the possibilities of what I will say in response. However, I know that whatever I face, I will be guided by my instincts, strengths, and the lessons I've learned since Lynn and I began our relationship. Today is the first day of the rest of our lives together. We will never get this day back again, and must live each moment as if it were our last day.

In the past five years, I have learned more about myself than I could have learned from any textbook I've read and studied in school. The greatest lesson I've learned of all the life lessons is that "life is a marathon and not a sprint." I need to learn things in my time and not go by anybody else's clock. If every challenge I encounter going forward is not recognized and dealt with, I cannot lead with confidence and perseverance. I need to be able to think things through and not get emotional about events occurring, of which I have no control. I need to solve problems the right way, not just my way.

Despite everything happening today, I will avoid making the mistake again of abandoning my employees and not giving them direction and guidance on where they need to follow, in the short and long-term strategic plan of Differencia. I have 11,000 employees in my charge. They're stationed in different parts of the globe. Many of these employees have families, children, and needs like me. I can always remember them. I am thinking less myopically and realizing that every decision I make as CEO either adds or subtracts value from the well-being of all those that report to me.

As we advance, starting today, I must take the news from Dr. Pereira, and digest it as a part of life. Life is not designed to be perfect, whatever "perfect" is. I realize today that true leaders are far from perfect, by design rather than intent. Attaining perfection is not the goal of a true leader. True leaders aim to become the best versions of themselves while helping others do the same.

Once we get settled in this afternoon, Lynn and I will have lunch together, and then pick Jessica up from school to tell her the news. I have blocked my schedule off for the day, and will be back to work tomorrow morning, unless there is an emergency.

We walk upstairs to our spacious townhouse after parking my car in the garage. I ask Lynn what she might want for lunch. She does not respond and gives me a blank stare. I thought she might be having another episode, but this was not the case. She walks up to me and puts her arms around my waist and hugs me so very tight. "Josh, just hold me and tell me it's going to be OK. Tell me that this is all a dream and I am going to wake up in my old job at Differencia. Please Josh, make it go away." I feel the wetness from her tears through my shirt. Suddenly I feel the calm I always feel when a crisis peaks after a panic attack. However, this time I did not panic. I stayed calm.

"Lynn, I will never let you go. I will support you wherever you are and whatever you do. You complete me and I need you to help me take on the biggest role I have ever had in my life." She slowly loosens her grip around my waist. She dries her eyes with her shirt sleeves and looks at me with absolute radiance. I haven't seen her glowing this much, since I asked her to be my wife.

"Josh, I love you so much, but I am afraid you can't do this job alone as the CEO. I just don't want you to get hurt. I know the pressures of the job, and I can't bear to see the company vultures crushing you with all types of unreasonable demands and deadlines you can't meet. I am so afraid for you, Josh."

I have never seen Lynn act like this before, exposing her most inner fears and trembling in fear before me like a mother protects her child. I am wondering if this is related to her diagnosis and recent behavior this morning, before we met with Dr. Pereira. I grow more concerned by the minute as she continues to discuss this very unusual dialog with me shortly before lunch.

Finally, Lynn grabs me by the hand and sits with me in the dining room, after grabbing some tissues to dry her eyes completely. "I am OK now, Josh. I am together now and had to get that out, between us. You need to decide if you want the job as CEO, because I can't do it. This is obvious. The job could kill me and destroy our family. I have no control over the matter as you could see by my behavior this morning."

I am now facing the Lynn that I know and trust. At least for now, she is lucid and on point with her words. Finally, she looks at me and says, "Well Josh, do you or do you not want the job?" I need to contact Dr. Mulcahy, as Board Director, and deliver my letter of resignation. I need to do this soon, to maintain continuity and trust in our organization. We need strong leadership wherever we decide it's best to get it."

I look up at Lynn and give her a blank stare. "What is that supposed to mean, wherever we get it?" She responds "It means exactly that, nothing more, nothing less. All I am saying is that we need to bring it to the Board, and let them know what my decision is; and we need to do it as soon as possible, to maintain stability in the company."

I am now having second thoughts on whether Lynn thinks that I can do this job. I am feeling as if she doubts my ability to lead. "Lynn, are you doubting my ability to lead Differencia? Do you think that I can't run the company as effectively and efficiently as you can? Where are you going with your comments?"

Lynn places her head in her hands, looks up at me remorsefully and says quietly, "Josh, I didn't mean for you to take it the wrong way or hurt your feelings. I truly have your back and know the pressure you are under now. All I am saying to you is that this is a process that needs to play out, be prepared for that." I sit in silence as she continues.

"Josh, I must bring all of this to Dr. Mulcahy, the chairperson of our BOD. I need to tell her my prognosis, and more importantly, what recently happened in Dr. Pereira's office just before we had our appointment today."

My first reaction in responding to what Lynn just said is not to say anything to Dr. Mulcahy until we think about this further, perhaps sleep on it tonight. "Lynn, do you think it might be a good idea if we just sleep on this tonight and not say anything to Dr. Mulcahy until we truly decide how we are going to present your prognosis?"

"Josh, here you go thinking about yourself again, and not thinking about the good of the company, or me for that matter." I snap back at her "Lynn, what are you talking about? How dare you accuse me of thinking only of myself here and not about you and the company for that matter! What gives you the right to judge me in such a cruel and harsh way, when we are under all this pressure together?"

"Josh, I truly and deeply love you with my heart and soul. However, sometimes I don't know whether your head is buried in your butt! You remain an enigma to me. Here I am, losing my memory, my job, my dignity, and my livelihood all at once. I am trying to rationalize a strategy with you to tell the Board of Directors that I can no longer do my job in the capacity that I served, and look for alternatives to keep Differencia going, with a smooth transition from me to someone else who's going to run the company."

"So, Lynn, I suppose you want me to place a call to Dr. Mulcahy and schedule a meeting with her as soon as possible?"

"Actually Josh, that would be a really good idea. We need to maintain stability in the company and assure ourselves that we are on track to getting a CEO in the front office as soon as possible. You should know how important that is as my Co-CEO."

"Lynn, it's just that it will be so strange for you to not be there with me when I am running the company, to think through some of the most difficult situations. I need you to be there with me, even if I must make the decision alone. I need your support."

"Josh, you are being ridiculous. Just listen to yourself. Do you think this is how a CEO should act when facing a crisis?"

"What are you talking about, Lynn? I am just thinking about how all this should be presented to Dr. Mulcahy when we make our appointment."

"Josh, I am still on the BOD, and no one has advised me differently. Let me make the call. I'll do it first thing in the morning. If she is not available, then I will leave a message to call me back. Does that sit well with you, Josh?"

I nod to Lynn affirmatively as we leave together to pick up Jessica from school. She had a big exam today, in her accelerated math class. I am sure that she did well. She always does. She will be nine years old next year and is already doing algebra and geometry. Well, what can you expect from genius kids, anyway?

We are not late. Jessica is waiting for us and displays smiles all over her pretty face. She has her mother's emerald-green eyes and sharp wit about her. She runs toward us. Lynn opens the car door and Jessica jumps in her lap and immediately opens her backpack, pulling out her algebra test.

Jessica shouts "Mommy, I got the highest grade in my class, and the teacher put a star on my paper, see?" Lynn looks at the paper and it is on quadratic equations. She then looks at the grade and it is a C+.

Lynn responds, "Oh Jessica, I am so proud of you, baby! Isn't this great Josh?" I honestly don't know how to respond to a C+ as a great grade. I just don't get it. I reply, "Yes, this is great Jessica. Then I rebound. "Did anyone get an A or B in your class, Jessica?"

Jessica suddenly gets off Lynn's lap and jumps over her and gets in the back seat of the SUV. She is silent. She puts on her seatbelt and does not say a single word. She crosses her arms and starts rocking back and forth like she always does when she gets angry and frustrated.

Lynn signals me to start the car and we proceed to our townhouse, which is about a twelve-minute drive from Jessica's school. Still, Jessica does not say anything to either Lynn or me as we approach our townhouse. I jump in. "Jessica, anything else exciting happen at school today?" Jessica continues to be verbally unresponsive. Lynn, gives me a look as if to say, let it go.

We arrive at the townhouse and are ready to enter the garage. Jessica suddenly directs her attention to me, after unlocking her seatbelt. When I finally stop the vehicle, she begins speaking rather loudly but not ill-tempered. "Daddy, I am in a special class with special students, who are all as old as me learning eleventh grade algebra. C+ in my class at my age is more harder than someone in the eleventh grade that gets an A."

Lynn chimes in, "Josh, your daughter is giving talking points to answer the same questions you asked me before we came to pick her up from school. You need all the facts that go into a strategy before you strategize. Everything in life is relative to facts based on fundamental principles that measure our relationships to one another."

I look at Lynn in total amazement and observe profound intuition, which many call emotional intelligence, in what she is saying to me, relative to our "genius" child. Although Lynn and I need to make some life-altering decisions over the next few weeks based on Dr. Pereira's diagnosis, we need to act quickly to maintain stability and confidence in the company we built together, going from the darkness into the light. We have carried through the blueprint for a wonder drug that will slow and maybe even cure Parkinson's Disease in its early stages.

I get it now! Tomorrow, Lynn will call Dr. Mulcahy, and get an appointment with her ASAP.

Lessons Learned

Josh, Lynn and Jessica return to their townhouse after informing Josh's staff that he would return to his office mid-afternoon.

Josh is uncertain about his future, but believes his instincts, strengths, and lessons learned will foster his success.

Life is a marathon, not a sprint. Confidence and perseverance are the keys to successful decision-making .Josh must concentrate on his organization, his employees, and the needs of their families.

Leaders are not perfect, and true leaders do not strive for perfection. They attempt to become the best version of themselves, and assist others to become the best version of themselves.

Lynn asks Josh to assure her that everything will be ok.

Josh answers Lynn that he will support her in every way he can.

Lynn tells Josh that she is afraid that he will not be able to cope with the demands of the CEO position. She asks him if he is ready to accept the demands of the job.

Lynn reflects that she must inform the board that she will resign as Co-CEO, to reduce the stress in her life.

Josh wonders if Lynn doubts his ability to lead Differencia. He suggests that they defer a decision until the next morning.

Josh lashes out at Lynn for accusing him of only thinking about himself and ignoring the company.

Lynn urges Josh to schedule a meeting with Dr. Mulcahy, to maintain stability in the company and get a CEO in the corner office as soon as possible.

Josh articulates that he needs Lynn's support and guidance to be an effective CEO.

Lynn asserts that she will schedule a meeting with Dr. Mulcahy.

Josh and Lynn leave together to pick up Jessica from school. Jessica tells Lynn that she received the highest grade in her class on an algebra test.

Lynn tells Josh that he must strategize by exhibiting more emotional intelligence, i.e. the ability to perceive the external environment before acting.

Is Josh's uncertainty as to how to inform his employees about the current challenges facing Differencial reasonable? Should he be more decisive?

Do you agree with this statement: life is a marathon, not a sprint?

In your view, what are the key ingredients for successful decision-making?

Do you strive for perfection in your everyday life? Is this healthy? Are you willing to accept less than perfect outcomes?

Is Josh effective in convincing Lynn that he will fully support her, no matter what her future holds? Have you ever been asked for help from others in a similar circumstance? How did you react? Would you modify your behavior now?

Is Lynn's questioning that Josh can be an effective leader without her guidance and support justified? Is Josh overreacting to Lynn's comments?

Is Lynn's decision to inform Dr. Mulcahy and the board of her need to resign reasonable, or should her decision be deferred?

Have you ever procrastinated in making a similar decision?

Do you agree with Lynn's criticism that Josh only thinks about himself?

What is your assessment thus far of Josh as a leader? Where are you at this point in your life?

Is Jessica sugarcoating the fact that she only received a C+ plus on her algebra test? Do you agree with her assertion that a C+ is not that bad, given her peer group?

In leadership theory, emotional intelligence, that is being aware of the surrounding environment, is more important than technical skills. How would you assess Josh's emotional intelligence?

Key Leadership Qualities Identified

Passion - Striving toward a goal or objective with fervor and determination. It is often said that if you do what you love, you will never have to work a day in your life.

Humility - Recognizing one's limitations and accepting that we will all need help from others in achieving our personal and professional goals.Humility is a strength, not a weakness.

Vision - Being able to anticipate the future. Authentic leaders are able to foresee numerous outcomes from a decision. As hockey great Wayne Gretzky would say, "I go not to where the puck is but where the puck is going to be."

Perseverance - Continued effort to achieve something, despite difficulties, failure, or opposition. "I get up every time I fall. I either win or I learn.

Self-efficacy - The ability to achieve goals through effort and perseverance. It is the development of confidence and pursuing new challenges.

Self-esteem - The belief that one has the inner qualities necessary for goal achievement. It is reinforced by success. It is not self-bestowed.

Chapter 4
The Family

It is Tuesday, October 4th at 9:00 AM, and Lynn has just texted Dr. Mulcahy, to call her when she gets her first available moment. I have already left for the office at 8:15 AM to meet with my senior staff, to review the week's agenda. I am already tired of the week that has not even started yet. I don't think that it is rocket science to figure out that this is going to be a difficult week, with Lynn's breaking the news to Dr. Mulcahy about Dr. Pereira's prognosis and recommendations.

Life is a very complicated process. We try to simplify it and it keeps getting more complicated. Therefore, I think I'll leave it alone for the time being and let things play out all by themselves. I need to focus on the priorities of the company as well as the strategic goals. There are priorities in my agenda, and vice versa for those that report to me. I can't be expected to solve all the problems of the company myself. When Lynn was at the company and we were working together, no matter how difficult the situation was, we always found ways to resolve problems, even when they seemed to be out of control. Why does this have to change now, especially when I can show the BOD I am up for the job? I just need more time to work myself into the position and earn the respect of senior staff and their direct reports.

It's 9:17 AM and I have run into some road traffic, so I will be arriving a bit late for my 9:30 AM meeting with senior staff. My phone is ringing, and it is Lynn. Dr. Mulcahy must have called her back. I'll bring her in through Bluetooth. "Hello honey! I am stuck in a bit of traffic and might be a bit late for my meeting with senior staff this morning. I wish you were here with me." Lynn responds sharply, "Josh, you are always late for meetings. It's not just your agenda. It's also everybody else's you need to consider." I rebut to Lynn as I am driving into my designated spot in the executive parking lot. I notice that Lynn's designated spot as Co-CEO has been removed. I didn't say anything to her. "Lynn, I was caught up in traffic and I have no control over traffic."

There is silence on her end of the call. I check and see if she is still on the call. Then, Lynn finally says something. "Josh, you and I have an appointment with Dr. Mulcahy at 10:00 AM tomorrow morning. The BOD will meet Friday to vote on how to proceed forward with the CEO position, based on the outcome of our meeting yesterday with Dr. Pereira." There is silence on the phone, and I reply. "Lynn, did you tell Dr. Mulcahy anything about the appointment with Dr. Pereira yesterday?" Lynn responds, "Josh, of course not! Do you think I'm an idiot?"

I apologize to Lynn and tell her that I am very nervous about everything. There is silence once again on the phone. Finally, I tell Lynn that I have to get to my meeting, where I am already late, and will call her later in the day once I get a break from my agenda. While walking up to my meeting, I began to realize how intense the next 24 hours are going to be for me and Lynn. We have been through so much personally and professionally over the past five years together, and now we are being challenged with probably the biggest decision outside of getting married that we will make in our lives as husband and wife.

It is 9:43 AM and I am greeted by my senior staff as I apologize for my lateness due to traffic. They appear to be very forgiving and understanding. Yet, why would they not be since they reported to me, and I sign their paychecks.

Getting through the agenda items today has been extremely difficult. Every time I try to follow the agenda, my mind keeps returning to the meeting tomorrow morning that I am very much not looking forward to, for so many reasons, on so many levels. It nauseates me to think how uncomfortable this meeting will be. However, it needs to happen, sooner rather than later.

It is Wednesday, October 5th at 4:00 AM, and I have not yet fallen asleep. Lynn, although sleeping off and on throughout the night, appeared very unsettled when she did sleep at all. We are both anxious, nervous, and expecting the worst for our futures at Differencia.

It is now 6:00 AM, and Lynn opens her eyes, rubs them vigorously, looks at me and smiles. "Josh, you look as terrible as I feel. Did you sleep a wink all night?" I respond, "Lynn if I were to tell you that I slept like a baby, you would call me a liar. The truth is, I might've gotten an hour of sleep, but kept waking up abruptly every time I dozed off. I can't get all of this out of my head right now. However, what I do know is that we need to get through today, so we can figure out where we are going forward in our personal and professional lives." Lynn responds affirmatively and we get up out of bed, shower, and get dressed and groomed before having breakfast. Then, we need to get Jessica ready for school, as well as feed her breakfast. She usually gets up around 7:00 AM, and Lynn drives her to school by 8:15 for the 9:00 first bell. Jessica is in advanced classes with students that have measured in her IQ range.

We can't be late for anything today, especially for our meeting with Dr. Mulcahy, Chair of the BOD. We have just dropped Jessica off at school, and are on our way to Dr. Mulcahy's office for our 10:00 AM meeting. We have plenty of time to grab a little snack before we meet with Dr. Mulcahy; an hour to be exact. We can wind down, relax, and enjoy each other's company and just be, well, us for an hour or so.

We migrate to this little diner about ten minutes from Differencia and get ourselves a small booth in the corner, abutting two large windows that let in a lot of sunshine. Although this is the month of October in downtown Los Angeles, it is warm and sunny. I guess you could just feel good about the day. I have a good feeling today for us and just want to live in the present moment, staring into her emerald, green eyes. Despite everything she has been through, Lynn is as beautiful and radiant as the day we exchanged vows and promised eternal support and love for one another. Isn't this really all that matters in life? I realize how selfish I have been in the past. I have always protected myself from harm. What about everybody else, especially Lynn?

I grab both of Lynn's hands as I begin to discuss what we will say at our meeting. Lynn remains silent as she always does when I begin a conversation. She never talks over me. This is something I learned from her and have mastered quite well over the past few months. I get much better traction communicating this way, with my subordinates and business associates.

Suddenly, Lynn's cell phone rings and I continue to talk about our meeting. Lynn appears extremely agitated by the call and blurts out in a loud voice, "Josh will you just hush for a minute? I can't hear what is being said to me. It's not clear. I can't hear anything Josh, I can't hear anything." I try to calm Lynn down and gently take the phone away from her. She is sobbing and I thought she might be having another one of her episodes.

"Hello, this is Josh Keating, Lynn's husband. Who are you and what is going on?" Lynn did not have an episode. I hear nothing but static on the other end of the phone line. Finally, a voice comes on the phone. "Mr. Keating, this is Dr. Scholtz, Jessica's principal at the Schumann School for Advanced Children." I abruptly cut in. "Why are you calling? Did something happen to Jessica? Is she OK?"

Dr, Scholtz responds, "Jessica asked her teacher in her 9:00 AM math class if she could go to the bathroom before the first bell rang. Her teacher, Mrs. Ward, gave her permission. It is now 9:15 AM and she is nowhere to be found in the school. Usually, the students are let into the classroom at 8:45 AM and the teacher is already there to greet them. This gives the students time to get settled before class officially begins."

I respond, "Dr. Scholtz, OK, OK. Please get to the point!" I am now beginning to sweat and my heart is racing. "Mr. Keating, your daughter has been missing for over a half hour now, and we can't find her. We've alerted the police and have placed a lockdown on the school. You or Dr. Marconi need to get here ASAP. We have also notified the highway patrol and the California State Police as well."

My body is shaking, and I grab Lynn's arm with tears in my eyes. "Lynn, we must leave now. I will explain along the way." She responds, "Josh, what is going on? Please tell me." I tell her, "Jessica is missing from school, and we have to go there right away." Lynn looks at me, as tears are falling from her face, and she is enthralled with anguish. I respond to her, "Take a deep breath and know it will be all right. I promise I won't let anything happen to her." She responds, "Josh, as much as I would like to believe you, we won't know anything until we get there and find Jessica safe. Please stop trying to comfort me! We have been through so much and we will get through this as well, together."

I look at my watch and it is 9:35 AM. "Lynn, should we call Dr. Mulcahy to inform her what is going on, and that will not be able to make the meeting this morning at 10:00 AM? This meeting is crucial, since the board will be meeting on Friday this week to discuss our collective fates." Lynn responds harshly, "Josh, how dare you think about us at a time like this, when our daughter is missing! She could have been kidnapped? She might've hit her head on something and is bleeding out. I am thinking of all crazy things right now about Jessica, and you are thinking about Dr. Mulcahy!" Lynn is almost hysterical at this point and is screaming very loudly at me.

However, I cannot control my emotions at this point. I lash out in response to her comments. "Lynn, now you know firsthand what I felt like when you didn't get off that plane traveling from Boston a few years ago! You told me I was selfish. You told me I wasn't thinking about the 11,000 employees who were waiting for me to give them directions. You lectured me about responsibility and leadership. Does this sound familiar, Lynn?" Abruptly, she stops talking and grabs my hand. Her hand is trembling. "Josh, you are right. It was easy for me to criticize you. However, knowing somebody very close to you could not be there anymore by your side is devastating. It stops life as you know it in your tracks, and the possible consequences are unthinkable." I respond to her, "That's OK, Lynn. I now realize that two wrongs do not make a right. You were right: at the time you were missing, I should have called Dr. French and announced to her that you could not make the presentation of the Parkinson's drug as planned because of a family emergency and you had not yet arrived home. I just want you to know while you were just screaming at me, I was texting Dr. Mulcahy to tell her that we would be detained indefinitely, because it was reported that our daughter was missing at school."

Lynn smiles at me and we proceed to the school's parking lot, where we usually drop Jessica off in the morning before the first bell. It is now 9:46 AM. We are greeted by two police officers from the LAPD Highway Patrol and a state police officer. We are escorted into the school and sent immediately to Dr. Scholz's office.

Dr. Scholz opens the conversation after asking us to take a seat in front of his desk. "Josh, Dr. Marconi, I want to express our sincerest apologies for what has transpired this morning. Jessica is a very cooperative and stable student. Lately, she has been, let's say, somewhat agitated and aggressive toward her peers in the class. All these students have been handpicked as exceptionally bright. Some have a little higher and some a little lower IQs than their peers. In fact, most of them have a higher IQ than their teacher."

I interrupt him. "Dr. Scholz, why are you telling us all this? And what does this have to do with Jessica, missing as we speak?" He calmly responds, "Josh, your daughter is almost 9 years old, and she has the IQ of a grad student at Princeton University. Emotionally, she is below her age level and often has the propensity to think irrationally when she is agitated."

Lynn responds to him. "Dr. Scholz, did anything happen this morning in class, before she went to the bathroom?" He responds, "Dr.

Marconi, I could bring her teacher to our meeting for a few minutes. I have a teaching assistant in the classroom who can take over the class while we ask her these questions. Would you be amenable if she agrees?” Lynn and I both nod that we agree. He excuses himself and attempts to find Jessica’s math teacher. Within a minute, Mrs. Reed joins us at our meeting.

After we make our introductions, Dr. Scholz asks Mrs. Reed if she would be comfortable answering a few questions from us. She nodded in agreement. Lynn opens the dialogue. “Mrs. Reed, did anything happen this morning in class before Jessica requested a hall pass to go to the bathroom?” She appeared somewhat confused about the question being asked and requested clarification. Then she responded, “Dr. Marconi, Jessica has been a bit out of sorts these last few days. In fact, she must go to the bathroom several times during class. I thought perhaps she was doing this to try to get out of class. However, math is her favorite subject. This was highly unusual behavior for Jessica. She can’t wait to get into class and does not waste a moment to raise her hand to ask questions or to answer my questions. We are on algorithms right now. She loves the class!”

I jump in next. “Mrs. Reed, why do you think Jessica was taking so many bathroom breaks?” She looks at me with a blank stare and is at a loss for words. I follow up with another question. “Mrs. Reed, please try to remember anything that you observed that Jessica might have reacted to or have done before the last bathroom break when she was discovered missing." She looks at me, and before she can speak, I jump back into the conversation. "This is very important to try to remember. It may give us a clue of where she might have gone when she left the classroom this morning."

She thinks long and hard before responding. "Josh, the only thing that I can think of in the last time before Jessica went to the bathroom and was reported missing, she was holding a piece of paper, which had a poem she told me she wrote about her mother this morning." I respond to Mrs. Reed, "How did you know that is what she was holding?" She responds, "I simply asked her, and she told me."

I look at Lynn and she looks at me. At that moment our minds connected, and we both thought the same thing. Lynn gently looks up and meets Mrs. Reed's eyes. Lynn responds, "Josh, Dr. Scholz, Mrs. Reed, I think I know where to find my daughter. At our last PTA meeting, you said that you had a botanical garden on display. Jessica had an exhibit with some insects for a science fair in the garden, if memory serves me correctly." Dr. Scholz acknowledged that Lynn's memory was correct. She followed up by asking if the exhibits were still on display in the garden. Dr. Scholz also nodded affirmatively. Lynn then asked him if he would take us there.

Immediately, Dr. Scholz dismisses Mrs. Reed to her classroom and escorts us to the botanical garden where Jessica's exhibit was on display. We walked through the atrium of the exhibit hall all the way to the end, to Jessica's exhibit. There we found Jessica with the poem she had written, in her hand. She was singing to her display of spiders, surrounded by beautiful waterspouts, in the garden comprised of stones and lilacs with ivory all around. Jessica sees Lynn and runs into her arms. Jessica begins to cry. "I am sorry Mommy. I just could not stop thinking about you and what you sang to me when you woke up in the hospital. We sang the song together. She opened the poem and showed it to Lynn. It was "the itsy-bitsy spider."

I could not be mad at Jessica. She is a special child. Although she is a genius, her feelings, her instincts, not talking about her intuition, are off the charts. Our appointment with Dr. Mulcahy was rescheduled for tomorrow at 10:00 AM. Oh, one more thing: we asked Dr. Scholz if we could have permission to bring Jessica to our meeting with Dr. Mulcahy tomorrow. He consented with reservation.

Lessons Learned

Lynn texts Dr. Mulcahy to schedule a meeting with her.

Josh realizes that he must concentrate on the priorities of Differencia and its strategic goals.

Josh asks Lynn if she told Dr. Mulcahy about her appointment with Dr. Pereira the previous day. Lynn responds that this is a foolish question.

Upon reflection, Josh recognizes that he is currently challenged with the biggest decision of his life outside of getting married.

Josh meets with the senior staff. He is distracted by worrying about his meeting the next day with Dr. Mulcahy.

Josh confides in Lynn that he is quite concerned about the meeting with Dr. Mulcahy.

Lynn drives Jessica to school.

Josh and Lynn drive to a diner to discuss their upcoming meeting with Dr. Mulcahy.

Lynn receives a phone call from Dr. Scholtz, the principal of Jessica's school. He indicates that Jessica is missing from the school and that he wants Josh and Lynn to come to the school at once.

Lynn becomes frantic and Josh attempts to comfort her.

Lynn reprimands Josh for being concerned with the upcoming meeting with Dr. Mulcahy, and not being concerned about Jessica's whereabouts.

Josh takes umbrage with Lynn's criticism of him, and says that he is being sensitive to the interests of all parties, Jessica, and his meeting with Dr. Mulcahy.

Lynn apologizes to Josh for her harsh criticism of him.

Josh and Lynn arrive at Jessica's school.

Dr. Scholtz apologizes to Josh and Lynn about the uncertainty as to where Jessica has gone, and indicates that Jessica is below grade level emotionally.

Lynn asked Dr. Scholtz if anything happened before she left to visit the bathroom. Dr. Scholtz summons Jessica's teacher to his office.

Jessica's teacher indicates that she requested several times during class that she be allowed to visit the bathroom.

Mrs. Reed, Jessica's teacher, indicates that she was holding a piece of paper with a poem of prayer she wrote about her mother.

Lynn responds that she believes that Jessica went to the botanical garden on the school grounds, and requests that Dr. Scholtz take her there.

Dr. Schultz brings Josh and Lynn to the botanical garden and locates Jessica there, with the poem in her hand.

Jessica is crying and shows "the itsy-bitsy spider poem" to Lynn, as a reminder to her that she was very ill at some point in the past.

Josh and Lynn ask Dr. Schultz for permission to bring her to the meeting with Dr. Mulcahy. Dr. Schultz agrees with reservation.

Questions to Ponder

How can Josh remain focused on the meeting agenda with his staff and not be distracted? Do you find yourself distracted in meetings? How do you handle this?

Do you have a difficult time in maintaining your staff's attention during meetings? What do you do to captivate your audience's attention during meetings? Can you think of innovative ways to command attention?

Is Josh becoming overly stressed about the upcoming meeting with Dr. Mulcahy? How can he reduce his stress?

Is Lynn overreacting to Dr. Scholtz's message that Jessica is missing from school? How would you have reacted? What could have been done differently?

Is Dr. Scholtz being overly dramatic in his message that Jessica is missing from the school building?

Is Lynn's criticism of Josh, that he is more concerned with the meeting with Dr. Mulcahy than Jessica's whereabouts, justified? Would you have reacted in the same way as Josh? If not, how would you have reacted?

What do you think of Josh's response to Lynn's criticisms? Is it effective in reducing his anger? Would you have responded differently? If so, how would you have responded?

What is your assessment of Jessica's EQ; that is, her emotional quotient? Is it below grade level? What can be done to increase it?

Have you ever been faced with a situation in which a worker's whereabouts is unknown? If so, how did you handle it? What are some of the ways you could handle it without being intrusive?

Should Josh and Lynn bring Jessica to the meeting with Dr. Mulcahy? Why or why not? What are the pros and cons of their decision?

Key Leadership Qualities Identified

Focus - The primary source of attention and effort. Decisions are based upon the end result desired. Olympic athletes are known for their focus on the goal to be attained.

Purpose - The value system upon which decisions are based. It is the inner moral compass which dictates one's daily actions. Without purpose, one's life has no meaning or direction. "If you do not know where you are going, any road will get you there."

Acceptance - Recognizing the environment which one is facing and responding accordingly. "Grant me the serenity to change the things I can, accept the things I can't, and the wisdom to know the difference."

Multi-Dimensional Thinking - Recognizing all possible outcomes from a decision, and developing contingency plans for each outcome. "The future belongs to those who prepare for it."

Admission of Mistakes - Recognizing a faulty decision and learning from it. "I get up every time I fall. I either win or I learn."

Emotional Quotient - Being aware of the environment in which one is operating. It measures how successful one is in responding to external circumstances.

Mentorship - Guiding others by assisting them in achieving their goals and objectives. Listening to others who have been successful in their personal and professional lives and following their insights.

Chapter 5

The Company

It is Wednesday, October 5th, 2022, at 9:00 AM. This time, Jessica is with me and Lynn. She took, with permission from her principal, a day off from school to be with us when we meet with Dr. Mulcahy. We returned to the same diner where we attempted to have breakfast yesterday morning and were quickly summoned away by an urgent phone call. The waitress recognized us and she smiled as she sat us in the same booth we were in yesterday, except now Jessica is between us. We hope for no other emergencies this morning, before our meeting with Dr. Mulcahy at 10:00 AM.

We are enjoying a hearty breakfast of French toast, eggs, sausages, and bacon, with a side of pancakes. It is 9:35 AM and we are 10 minutes from Differencia. Jessica and I are smiling. Lynn is quite melancholy and very quiet as we arrive at Dr. Mulcahy's office. It is now 9:55 AM and she opens her office door and is quite surprised to see Jessica. We did not tell her that Jessica was coming to our meeting. Dr. Mulcahy was very cordial and took Jessica beside her and asked her if she would sit quietly for a minute while she spoke to her mother and father. Dr. Mulcahy asked her if she would like to use her iPad, where she had some very interesting word puzzles that needed to be solved. She directed Jessica to the app on her iPad which contained the word puzzles. Jessica took it, smiled at Dr. Mulcahy, and quietly took a seat in the atrium which led to Dr. Mulcahy's office. Jessica knew something was up and is quite a quick study, knowing her place at the proper time.

Dr. Mulcahy came over to me and Lynn and asked why we brought Jessica to our meeting. We told her that the principal, Dr. Scholz, had given us permission to take her to the meeting. She smiled, shook her head, and then stated in a rather low but firm voice, "You guys know that what we discuss is totally in confidence, and no one should hear what we say outside our circle. We have a fiduciary obligation to our board members and our employees to keep things confidential."

Lynn looks at Dr. Mulcahy most despondently, and was disappointed in her comments projected toward Jessica. Her face showed contempt toward Dr. Mulcahy, but not as an employee or a board member. Rather, her emotions were directed to Dr. Mulcahy as a mother whose child was just attacked and ridiculed. I found this to be a very awkward moment between them. I wasn't sure whether I should step in at this point and say something, as I felt the same way as Lynn when Dr. Mulcahy was making her comments projected toward Jessica.

Lynn finally chimes in, "Bonnie, she is our family and what we tell you, she already knows. So, what is the big deal if we bring her to our meeting? She is not going to be giving away trade secrets for money. Is she?"

Dr Mulcahy delays her response. She looks down at her freshly vacuumed carpet in her plush office, and smiles in a cynical fashion.

"This has nothing to do with family, Lynn. This is about business, and you can't mix the two together. This would be like mixing water and sulfuric acid. Temperatures will rise and violent results will occur if not handled properly. You get the point, Lynn?" Dr. Mulcahy pauses, takes a deep breath, and continues. "Jessica is not an employee of Differencia. As much as you love your child, which I understand, you cannot mix business with family life. It looks bad with our Board of Directors, especially where we are deciding on our CEO positions and the fate of the entire company."

Lynn is speechless and I chime into the conversation. "Bonnie, after all we've done together at Differencia to get to this point. Does it really come down to this, Jessica's confidentiality with her mother's fate? And, might I add, my fate with this company?" I can hear my voice beginning to tremble as I begin to perspire and hyperventilate. I loosen my tie and sit down on Dr. Mulcahy's visiting chair behind her desk. Lynn calls out to me as I hear her voice in the distance, as it slowly fades from my consciousness.

The next thing I know is that I am being transported from the ER at Los Angeles Medical Center to intensive care with all types of tubes sticking in and out of my body, let alone an oxygen mask secured to my nose and mouth. "What is going on? Where are you taking me?" Lynn and Jessica are by my side and look horrified. The attendant responds, "Your room in intensive care, Mr. Keating. You had a serious heart attack, and we almost lost you twice. The cardiologist will be in shortly to explain to you, once they get you settled."

Lynn is looking at me in horror abutting shock, and the tears are flowing from Jessica's face as they wheel me into the ICU cardiac unit of The Los Angeles Medical Center. They finally got me settled into a bed in the ICU and closed the curtain around my bed. Jessica and Lynn are with me, and are both holding both my hands as we wait for the cardiologist. It took only ten minutes for Dr. Martinez to arrive, who wore a wrinkled white lab jacket that looked like he had slept in it for two days. He was bald on top of his head, yet had a grayish white ponytail wrapped in an elastic, and a black moustache. I was too drugged to notice anything else about him. Yet, I was lucid enough to listen to him.

"Mr. Keating, my name is Dr. Louis Martinez. I am the chief resident cardiologist here at the medical center, called here by my close friend and colleague, Dr. Bonnie Mulcahy. She apparently had it arranged to have you sent here ASAP. And it is a good thing her wishes became a reality. To that point, I would also like to note that Dr. Mulcahy is the reason you are speaking to me in the present moment."

Again, I am loaded up with drugs, but I continue to listen to Dr. Martinez. "Mr. Keating, do you know what ventricular fibrillation is?" I nod my head back and forth indicating that I don't know what it is. "Ventricular fibrillation is an unstable and irregular heart rhythm, in which the ventricle chambers of the heart quiver and can lead to cardiac arrest and no pulse in a matter of minutes, sometimes seconds, unless immediate medical attention can restore the heart to a normal rhythm."

I signal with my hands for the doctor to continue. "In your case, Joshua, less than an hour ago, you had a heart attack which caused the ventricles in the lower chambers of your heart to quiver, causing an unstable arrythmia which left you unconscious in a matter of seconds. Dr. Mulcahy, as a medical doctor, recognized the symptoms right away. She immediately applied CPR to your chest, trying to stimulate your heart after calling 911. You were not responding, but still had a faint pulse." Dr. Martinez then takes a quick breath and continues. "Dr. Mulcahy then grabbed the defibrillator in the atrium outside her office, and immediately continued treatment to your heart. Shortly thereafter, the EMTs arrived and took you here to the LA Medical Center cardiac unit. Then, she called me. Here I am."

We are going to watch you for the next 24 to 48 hours, to make sure your heart beats normally, and so we have a chance to test the enzymes in your blood to make sure there was no further damage to your heart. We will keep you posted, as well as keep your family apprised as to what is going on. I understand that Mrs. Marconi is your health care proxy."

I hear Lynn talking to Dr. Martinez and I am very sleepy. This is the last thing I remember before I was sitting up, eating Jell-O and dry, mushy hospital food after they moved me to a semiprivate room.

It is now Thursday, October 20th. This afternoon at 3:00 PM, I will be meeting with Dr. Martinez, Dr. Pereira, Lynn, Dr. Mulcahy, and yes, my daughter Jessica, to discuss my prognosis and future healthcare plan. Lynn has been meeting with Dr. Mulcahy since my heart attack just about two weeks ago, while I went from intensive care to regular hospital care for follow-up and cardiac rehabilitation. I will be brought up to date today on everything in the hospital conference room, as I am waiting to get discharged today.

Lynn and Jessica arrived at 1:00 PM, as I have been waiting for this day for two weeks. Isolated from the rest of the world, while I was healing and rehabilitating from my near-death experience. The interesting part in all of this is that the lack of communication with the outside world, outside my family, was refreshing and invigorating to my mental health and physical stamina overall. Life took on a whole new meaning and I realized – you could be the most important person in the world, possess all the wealth on the planet, and everybody could love you or hate you. All of this means nothing because you could be gone in seconds from all this reality around you, if your heart stops beating and you flatline in the presence of everybody you know and care about.

In a previous employment in Boston, Massachusetts, I saw my boss drop dead in front of me in a matter of seconds, and I couldn't do anything about it. This time, it could've been me. I have a second chance and I don't want to give it away over a job. I want my life back. However, this time it will be on my terms. I couldn't bear to think what it would be like if I could not see my daughter Jessica grow up. I couldn't bear the thought of Lynn not having anyone to care for her through her life-threatening illnesses, and raising a genius child by herself. I want my family back more than I want to be the CEO of a billion-dollar pharmaceutical company.

Prior to our meeting today, Jessica, Lynn and I will go to the hospital cafeteria and get some "hospital food" which I hopefully will not have to eat after I leave this place. I will need healing from my "healing" if you know what I mean.

As always, Jessica and Lynn are happy to see me and overjoyed that I am coming home today, after our meeting with Dr. Mulcahy and the doctors to decide where we will go next. Lynn and I decided that we would give permission for Dr. Mulcahy, Dr. Pereira, and Dr. Martinez to share information transparently with our medical records. Going forward will be crucial from a medical standpoint, both personally and professionally, for Lynn, Jessica, and myself.

Lessons Learned

Lynn, Josh, and Jessica meet in a diner located on the route to Dr. Mulcahy's office. After breakfast they leave for their meeting with Dr. Mulcahy.

Dr. Mulcahy expresses surprise to see Jessica. Jessica senses that something is not right.

Dr. Mulcahy is concerned that having Jessica attend the meeting is a violation of fiduciary confidentiality.

Lynn reacts with disdain that Jessica's presence at the meeting is a violation of confidentiality.

Dr. Mulcahy responds that since Jessica is not an employee of Differencia, she should not be allowed to attend the Board meeting. Lynn remains adamant in her position that Jessica be allowed to attend the meeting.

Josh has a seizure and is transported to the ER at the Los Angeles Medical Center, and is transferred to the ICU cardiac unit. He is told he has experienced a serious heart attack.

Josh is greeted by Dr. Louis Martinez, the chief resident cardiologist at the Los Angeles Medical Center. He tells Josh that he has experienced severe ventricular fibrillation, an unstable irregular heart rhythm. Dr. Mulcahy restored Josh's heart rhythm and summoned an ambulance to take him immediately to the hospital.

Lynn, Josh, and Jessica meet with Dr. Martinez, Dr. Pereira, and Dr. Mulcahy.

Josh realizes that family relationships are more important than career success. He must reorient his lifestyle.

Lynn and Josh agree to give permission to Dr. Mulcahy, Dr. Pereira and Dr. Martinez to make their medical records transparent.

Questions to Ponder

Do you agree with Dr. Mulcahy that allowing Jessica to attend the meeting represents a breach of confidentiality? Why or why not? Have you ever faced a similar circumstance in your career?

Is Lynn's reaction to Dr. Mulcahy's assertion reasonable? Why or why not? How would you have reacted?

What argument would you have made to convince Dr. Mulcahy to allow Jessica to attend the meeting?

Is the reality that Jessica is a nine-year-old and not likely to gossip about the company's business a relevant factor in allowing her to attend the meeting?

Is Josh overreacting to the conflict between Dr. Mulcahy and Lynn, about allowing Jessica to attend the meeting?

Do you think that Josh's heart attack sent a signal to him that to maintain his family responsibilities, he must adjust his lifestyle? Have you had a medical emergency that required a modification of your lifestyle? What was the result?

Are you willing to share your medical records with your doctors, so they can assess your capability of fulfilling your job functions? If not, why not?

Key Leadership Qualities Identified

Fiduciary Responsibility - The financial responsibility that an organization has to their stakeholders. Engaging in activities that promote an organization's profitability subject to the legal environment .

Fiduciary Confidentiality - Making sure that an organization's business decisions are protected from public view. It is a necessary condition to maintain a competitive advantage. The prohibition of insider trading is a good example.

Situational Ethics - Recognizing there are no moral absolutes. It allows a drug to be brought to market before exhaustive testing if it has the possibility to improve a patient's quality of life. The promising Alzheimer's drug is an excellent example.

Health Transparency - Sharing one's medical records with one's employer, so as to make transparent one's capability to perform one's duties. It places the needs of an organization above those of the individual.

Chapter 6

Reflection Before Perception "The Homecoming"

My family drove me to our townhouse in LA, after I stayed two weeks in the hospital after an unexpected near-death experience, which included a heart attack triggered by an undetected cardiac condition described to me as ventricular fibrillation. Dr. Mulcahy saved my life. I will never forget that and be grateful to her forever.

Apparently, all those times I thought I was getting anxiety attacks and never going to the doctor to have these episodes checked out were described to me as episodes of ventricular fibrillation, where the chambers of my heart quiver or something that causes me to get an irregular heartbeat, which can lead to cardiac arrest. I don't even know if I am explaining it right. However, what I do know is that I almost died because I didn't take care of myself, when all I could think about was my work. I neglected my child, my wife and business partner, and most of all, myself! How could I look after everyone else when I needed to look after myself first?

Once we got settled and snacked on some lunch we bought on the way home, I asked Lynn the following question: "Do you think that I am a bad person? I mean, do you think I am a failure on purpose?" She looks at me as if she is staring at a three-headed dragon with advanced dementia. "Josh, what in creation are you talking about? You are not making any sense." Jessica is calmly sitting on the kitchen stool, munching on a slice of pizza and washing it down with some soda. She appears to not be paying any attention to our dialog.

"Lynn, it is always me that messes things up, and everything always goes wrong because I am so insecure and inept. I am always holding on to your coattails and always try to get the credit when you figure things out when I can't." She is now looking at me with fire in her eyes and blurts out "Stop it, Josh! Stop being the victim. If you want me to sympathize with you on this one, I won't!" She continues. "Josh, I am not your guardian angel, your mother, or your appeaser. I am your wife and the mother of your child. Don't you get it? I will not give you sympathy."

Lynn's eyes are now filling with moisture, and I am beginning to perspire. This was the first thing that happened to me in Dr. Mulcahy's office before I passed out. I try to remain calm and just remembered it was time for me to take my blood pressure medication. I will be monitored over the next three months to determine if I need an implantable cardioverter-defibrillator. This is when I am scheduled for my next visit with the cardiologist.

After I take my medication and drink a tall glass of water, Lynn apologizes to me for getting me upset. She is aware I need to rest and continue rehabilitating at home, until I am ready to return to work. Jessica is going to do her homework now. We will have supper, and then Lynn and I will discuss her meetings with Dr. Mulcahy over the past two weeks. Perhaps, we can just do this tomorrow morning. Tuesday, October 25th, the three of us (Dr. Mulcahy, Lynn and I) will meet in Dr. Mulcahy's office to discuss what she will tell the Board on Friday, October 28th, at the 10:00 AM call to order. Lynn and I will be present. We do not plan on taking Jessica, as we are working in her best interests.

It is now 5:35 PM and we all had a rough day. Supper is finished early, and Jessica is doing her homework quietly in her room. However, she has a great set of supersonic ears that hear even the slightest movements in the sound bites traveling between Lynn and me when we are in the kitchen.

I hear the door opening in her room, as she creeps slowly and meticulously into the kitchen to get a drink of water (as she says). Suddenly, she turns to me and Lynn and smiles in a very crafty and mysterious manner, posturing her body between us, sitting on the love seat in the great room of our townhouse.

I look at Jessica and ask, "What's up sweetheart? Did you finish your homework?" Jessica does not answer and starts rocking back and forth, staring at her shoes as she gets agitated. I ask her once again, "What's up baby girl? Is there something bothering you?" She poises herself with that same mischievous smile and smirks as me. Then she shows the same body language to Lynn as she continues sitting between us.

I can sense the calm before the storm here with our little girl, and so does Lynn, sensing the same heaviness of unsettled karma brewing in the air at the present time. Finally, Jessica says to me in a low, determined, almost commanding voice, "I hear you guys don't want to take me to your meeting with Dr. Mulcahy next Tuesday." Lynn cuts in sharply and says, "We don't want you to miss school, Jessica." She begins rocking back and forth once again, staring at the floor, and says in a very determined, emotional tone, "Mommy, don't lie to me. For once tell me the truth. Stop lying to yourselves about the truth. Stop lying to everybody about what is going on in our house."

I stare at Lynn in such astonishment and can't believe what is coming out of the mouth of this child. Her insight is off the charts, and I was so busy working all these years that I never took the time to really understand that what Lynn and I have created together is our legacy, Jessica. I now realize that she is a combination of my weaknesses, which are Lynn's strengths; and Lynn's weaknesses, which are my strengths.

Jessica grabs both of our hands, mine with her left hand and Lynn's with her right, moving her head back and forth, looking at Lynn and me with tears in her eyes, finally blurting out "Mom and Dad, you can't have your meeting on Tuesday without me, because I am the part of you that will be missing in your meeting, and your decision next Friday will stay with you for the rest of your life."

I look at Jessica most tenderly as I let her hand go. Lynn follows suit, doing the same. I respond, "Baby girl, God has gifted you with incredible insight and the ability to read into our feelings. You made me think of things, feel things, I have never been able to feel before.

You are amazing. You are a genius. You are still our little girl." Lynn is speechless as Jessica gets up from the loveseat and goes back to her room to finish her homework.

Tomorrow, we will discuss our meeting with Dr. Mulcahy on Tuesday, and Jessica will be with us. Good night to our readers and on to Chapter 7!

Lessons Learned

Lynn and Jessica bring Josh home to their townhouse in Los Angeles after his two week stay in the hospital.

Josh's episodes of anxiety were symptomatic of ventricular fibrillation. This serves as a warning to him that he must balance his personal and professional life.

Josh asks Lynn if she thinks he is a bad person. Lynn ignores Josh's question.

Josh declares that he is insecure and inept. He portrays himself as a victim. Lynn does not sympathize with Josh for upsetting him.

Lynn and Josh planned to meet with Dr. Mulcahy in her office, to discuss the CEO position. They do not plan on taking Jessica.

Jessica joins Josh and Lynn in the kitchen. She sways back and forth in her shoes and has a grim look on her face.

Jessica tells Josh and Lynn that she is aware that they do not want to bring her to the meeting with Dr. Mulcahy.

Jessica responds that since she is an integral part of the family, she should be allowed to attend the meeting.

Lynn and Josh recognize the importance of having Jessica attend the meeting with Dr. Mulcahy, and agree to have her attend the meeting.

Questions to Ponder

Have you ever experienced episodes of stress similar to those experienced by Josh? How did you react? Were they symptomatic of ventricular fibrillation? If so, did you modify your behavior?

In your view, does Josh have a victim mentality? Does he feel he is continuously controlled by external circumstances? Have you ever experienced this pattern of thinking? What effect did it have on your ability to make a successful decision?

Is Lynn's decision not to be an enabler to Josh a good one?

Have you ever been an enabler to others to reinforce their bad habits? What can you do to become a mentor and not an enabler?

Is Jessica's reaction to Josh and Lynn's decision to not have her attend the meeting justified? Have you ever made the decision not to include a family member in a meeting because you feel it was not in their best interests? Do you regret that decision?

Were Lynn and Josh wise to recant their decision to exclude Jessica from the meeting with Dr. Mulcahy? Have you revisited a decision in similar circumstances?

Key Leadership Qualities Identified

Stress reduction - Effective leaders control the stress they are confronted with in their day-to-day activities. They realize that mild stress leads to effective decision making, but that excessive stress defeats the ability to think clearly.

Mindfulness Meditation - Focusing on being keenly aware of what you're sensing and feeling in the moment, without interpretation or judgment. The daily practice of this leads to stress reduction and improved decision making.

Developing Positive Mantras - A word or phrase to repeat during meditation. It is often used to increase self-esteem and self-efficacy. "I can accomplish anything I set my mind to."

Bulldog Mentality - The belief that one has control over their destiny, and that being proactive maximizes the probability of success in one's endeavors. One responds to the challenges of everyday life by saying "I can do this."

Participative Decision-Making - Incorporating numerous opinions when making a decision. It often leads to diverse perspectives on an issue, and invariably leads to better decisions.

Tolerance - Listening to the opinions of others. It fosters relationship-building and the development of trust. It recognizes that each individual has a unique set of skills.

Chapter 7
Family Values and Corporate Obligations

It is Friday, breakfast time on October 21st, and Jessica, I and Lynn are having a laughing fit in the kitchen while we are eating our bacon, eggs, and sausages, prepared by our favorite chef, "Mommie" Lynn. Apparently, "Daddy" came down to breakfast wearing two different socks. They immediately bring this to my attention as I stare down at my shoes and notice the stark difference between the two pairs of socks. Usually, I would get all bent out of shape thinking they were making fun of me, and strike an "attitude" with both Lynn and Jessica for the rest of the day.

This morning it was different. We laughed and really, after a very long time, enjoyed ourselves as a family. Our laughter was genuine, sincere, and inclusive. I wish you could be there to see us all laughing together and enjoying each other's company as one happy family. I don't ever remember doing that when I was working. My only focus was my agenda for the day, the traveling I would have to do that week, and the meetings I would have to forgo to attend more meaningful meetings. Thinking of my family was the last thing on my mind when it should have been my first.

It is almost time to take Jessica to school, and Lynn is going to drive her there today. I will stay home and do the dishes from breakfast. This is really a change from my 14-hour-per-day schedule, sometimes with little or no sleep between each day. I don't know how I did this.

I am beginning to understand how I took ill. My condition didn't happen suddenly. It developed over a period of years. I lost track of where I was going and why I was getting to where I wanted to go. Was it only to earn money? Was it to protect my fragile ego? Was it to convince myself that I'm the smartest man on the planet, and could solve every problem on my own? Was I trying to appease my lack of social skills? I am thinking about all of these questions as I am here at the kitchen sink, washing my breakfast dishes.

Before I realize the time, Lynn is already back from driving Jessica to school for her first bell at 8:00 AM. Lynn comes in the door, smiling and ready to sit down in the great room with me to talk about Dr. Mulcahy and our futures at Differencia, and our new lifestyle here at home as a family, until the verdict is decided on how and if we are ever going to work at Differencia again.

We are financially solvent and will never have any money problems, even if we live to be 100 years old. We have a trust fund set up for Jessica and a Will that will protect her for the rest of her life. Her inheritance will be great, based on our legacy and hard work over the past 25 years of our working lives.

Lynn brought home a couple of lattes for us to enjoy while we are having our discussion this morning, and a couple of Danish pastries, which I am not supposed to have, by the way, due to my cardiovascular condition. However, our discussion can be an exception, and I will be careful what I eat for the remainder of the weekend.

It is approximately 9:00 AM. Lynn and I are getting ready to begin our discussion about our meeting with Dr. Mulcahy next Tuesday when a call comes in from Jessica's psychologist at her school. Gifted children who go to Jessica's school in LA are periodically assessed psychologically for any changes in their learning patterns and behavior. They want to be very careful not to put any additional stress on these children, and determine if they are going too far when setting the bar higher, giving them more challenging tasks and problems solving exercises in their studies. They don't want to put these gifted children into psychological turmoil and shut them down academically. This could cause a permanent setback in their education.

Lynn answers the phone. "Hello, this is Dr. Minerva Jones from the Putt Institute for Gifted Children. I am calling you regarding your daughter Jessica. Do you have a moment to speak?" Lynn gives me a blank stare and hands her cell phone to me to talk to Dr. Jones. I immediately throw my hands in the air, not knowing what this is all about. I take the phone, and I answer the call. "Who is this, please?" There is a 5-second pause. "This is Dr. Minerva Jones, the chief psychologist at Jessica's school. I thought I would be speaking to Dr. Marconi. Are you related to Jessica?" I immediately feel my blood pressure rising and can't think of why I must answer such a ridiculous question. I sharply respond, "I am her father. Is this relationship enough for you to talk to me?" Lynn is now gesturing to me with her hands moving up and down, for me to take it easy and not take the question personally. Dr. Jones responds, "I apologize; who am I speaking to again?" I immediately respond, "This is her father, Joshua Keating." Dr. Jones responds, "Mr. Keating, we need to be very careful whom we are speaking to at any given moment, as there are stringent HIPAA laws that we must abide by."

I try to keep myself calm. However, I respond to her in a less-than-amicable manner. I really can't help myself here. "Dr. Jones, I am well aware of HIPAA laws, as I oversee a $20 billion company with over 11,000 employees globally." There was a pause on the phone for about 10 seconds. Finally, she responds to my last comment. "Mr. Keating, I am not questioning the integrity and magnitude of your profession as a leader of thousands of employees. I am merely focusing on my concern for your daughter Jessica." Lynn is gesturing to me with her hands to get on with the conversation. I finally pull myself together and focus on what Dr. Jones has to say. I put Lynn's cell phone on speaker mode and lay it down on the coffee table in the great room. I let her know that I have Jessica's mother on the phone with me, as she explains the reason for her call.

"Mr. Keating, we recently did a series of psychological tests, supervised by me as a neuropsychologist, on your daughter. In recent weeks, most recently in the past week, Jessica has exhibited some very unusual behavior." I immediately interrupt her and ask what she means by very unusual behavior. She continues. "An example I can give you, Mr. Keating, is last Thursday, during second-period pre-algebra class; Jessica began screaming the answers to her second problem so loudly in class that I had to have her excused and taken out of the classroom by the class monitor until she calmed down. The class was pretty shaken up, as was the instructor, by her behavior." Lynn and I look at each other in total astonishment at Jessica's reported behavior.

I asked Dr. Jones to continue. "Two weeks ago, Friday, before third-period dance class, Jessica lay motionless on the hallway floor for about 10 minutes before coming to class. She walked into the classroom as if it had never happened. When we asked her for an explanation, she just smiled and kept walking away from us. We didn't pursue it any further." My first reaction to Dr. Jones was to ask her why she didn't say anything about this to us until now. She admittedly shared with us that gifted children sometimes display abnormal, acting-out behaviors within their age group. Many times, the symptoms disappear as they are just trying to grapple for attention.

My question to Dr. Jones is, why the call now? What did she see in Jessica that prompted this call to us this morning? This was her response. "Mr. Keating and Dr. Marconi, I have been a neuropsychologist for over 20 years. Often, I trust my instincts when I observe behavior that is not just bizarre, but physiologically and psychologically challenging in my profession to observe. I don't want to alarm you, but based on my observation of Jessica's behavior over the past several weeks, I think she could be autistic." My reaction to Dr. Jones was one of shock and dismay. Lynn looks at me with astonishment and grief, and her eyes immediately begin to fill with moisture. However, she remained silent as I continued the conversation.

I am now beginning to feel the calm and the focus reverberating through my body, as often happens after I peak a very stressful period. I ask Dr. Jones what the next steps might be. "Mr. Keating, we would like to do a series of tests on Jessica to determine if she is indeed autistic, and if so, where she is on the spectrum." I tell her that it was my understanding that autistic children usually have a very low IQ. How is it that Jessica has an IQ of a genius and possibly could have autism? "Mr. Keating, very gifted children with high IQs can also be autistic. In fact, the behaviors they exhibit have to do with very complicated neurological patterns, many of which we are only beginning to understand. Let's just do the tests first, if you agree, and get an accurate diagnosis. We will know more at that time about Jessica's behavior, and then be better equipped to handle it."

I ask Dr. Jones if Jessica will be taken out of school. "Mr. Keating let's take one step at a time. We need to tell Jessica that she must go through a series of tests for her good. It will help all of us deal with her problems effectively. At this point, we have no intention of pulling her out of school, until we know more about her situation. Every child is different. We understand, and we respect that to be true. In the meantime, everything at her school will remain normal. Are you willing to schedule a day we can test her?"

Lynn and I agree to make an appointment for Jessica, and Dr. Jones will get back to us on availability over the next few days. This is another personal challenge we must face. However, we will persevere through all of this. Each of us in our family have personal obstacles; we must get over them and face them with compassion, understanding, loyalty to each other, and dignity. This is a paradigm of core values that we as a family will challenge. We will face every conceivable obstacle together, no matter the consequences.

Although Lynn and I are sidelined in real-time physically, our prognosis before Dr. Mulcahy and our appearance as Co-CEOs one last time before the Board of Directors is molded by our core values and judgments as leaders, which will affect the livelihoods and futures of thousands of employees globally. It all begins with the family. Lynn and I continue our conversation about our meeting with Dr. Mulcahy on Tuesday, and our recommended next steps to her on our collective futures and the future of Differencia.

For the first time in my life, I am sitting next to my lifelong partner, business associate, the mother of my child and I am speechless. I don't know where to begin our conversation. Where do we go from here? I feel like time has placed us in some nexus of default, where the curtain has come down and we fade into oblivion, leaving behind an unfinished legacy without a successor.

Lynn is staring at me and looks concerned. "Josh, are you OK? Are you feeling alright? Do you need to take a break? I know the news we got on Jessica is hard to digest. However, we must deal with it just like every other crisis since we've known each other, plus the one coming up with Dr. Mulcahy." I apologize to Lynn and ask her if she would like to initiate the discussion.

Lynn faintly smiles at me and gently takes my hand as she glances at the carpeted floor in the great room of our condo. "Josh, we have medical issues that presently consume our existence twenty-four seven. I have neurological issues and you have cardiac issues. Both in their respective arenas are life threatening, primarily to us, and then to the organization within our charge, because we can't function in it."

I respond to Lynn, "I am stronger and feel much better. I can function as CEO at Differencia if I take my medications, keep my doctors' visits, and follow-up with my blood tests, etc." Lynn remains silent and lets me continue until I am ready to yield the conversation back to her. She does not let go of my hand while I am talking to her. When I finish talking, She shakes her head at me with that same faint smile and lets go of my hand.

"Josh, my love. Stop kidding yourself and be serious about one thing for once in your life. You have limits and there are boundaries around those limits. These boundaries are set for your own welfare and the welfare of those employees of Differencia, who trust you with their livelihood, their profession, and the hundreds of thousands of Differencia customers who use our drugs to stay alive." I look at her with astonishment and want to respond to her, but can't find the words.

Lynn looks at me tenderly and grabs my hand once again. "Josh, I love you more than you will ever know. I would end my own life to save your life. I love my daughter more than I love us both together, because she is a part of both of us. Are you getting this, Josh?"

I feel my lips quivering as my palms are beginning to sweat, and Lynn lets go of my hand once again. I finally respond. "I am scared. I don't want to be an invalid. I am too young to give this up. I have worked so hard to get where I am today. I cannot let go of this, Lynn. I just cannot let this go. You need to understand."

Lynn is staring at me right now as her face is beginning to flush. She is clearly angry at me and responds "Josh, you must be one of the most selfish individuals I've ever met in my life. It is always about you. It was about you from the first day that I met you. It was about you when Medical Solutions was misinformed about why I was missing. I don't even know where to begin anymore! When are you going to stop thinking about yourself and focus on the good of the many?"

At this point I am enraged by Lynn's accusations. I strike back at her. "I have done everything within my power to be a good provider, a good father, and what I thought was a decent CEO to Differencia. This is what I get in return, coming from the person closest to me?" I feel my heart beginning to race, and the room is beginning to spin. Her voice sounds to me like loud drums after having a hangover.

Finally, I put my hand up and say to her, "Stop! Please just stop! I don't want to fight anymore. I am a sick man, and I don't want to die. Differencia keeps me going, keeps me alive, and gives me hope to carry on my life."

Lynn responds, "Is that all that keeps you going in your life, Josh? What about me and Jessica? Don't we count here at all? You are our life, not Differencia." The tears are beginning to flow down her face, and for the first time in my life, I realize that she is right. As vital as I think myself to be of Differencia, I am missing the point about why I work there.

It makes me think back to Dr. Fringe at Medical Solutions. She came to the company from a very affluent family, had attended and graduated very highly-credentialed universities, and was at the top of her game and the company when she fell victim and orchestrated one of the biggest pharmaceutical scandals ever recorded. How does that happen? At one point she was the head of all research at Medical Solutions and chaired the BOD. It was Lynn and I that picked up the pieces of the scandal, figured it all out and started a new company with the approval of the BOD. What am I thinking? Why do I continue to put my ego above anything I believe to be the right thing to do? Why do I continue to beg loyalty to myself, before anything else on this planet that I love and cherish?

I respond to Lynn and offer my deepest apologies for "falling off the wagon" once again to protect my own ego. "Josh, you don't have to apologize to me anymore when you fail to mask your fears. I am part of you, and you are part of me. Don't you think I have the same fears? Don't you think I am as scared as you every morning that I wake up and I don't know where I am going to find myself?"

I can feel the tears mounting in my eye sockets and realize how selfish I have always been. I realize how I have masked my fears by throwing my weight around, just to protect my ego. This is not what leaders are supposed to do. They need to assess situations from all angles and make choices that may not include them, in order to bring a company forward and satisfy its strategic plan.

I have missed the boat on so many occasions by only listening to my inner voice, blocking everything out that suggested a better voice of reason. I even blocked out my family to lean on my egocentric attributes, to bully my way into having people think my way, even those closest to me. I am glad Lynn and I are finally coming to grips with our reality. Oh my gosh, I need to pick Jessica up from school. She has an early dismissal today at noon. There is a teacher's meeting. We have been here talking for almost three hours and have not yet decided on our strategy for next Tuesday's meeting with Dr. Mulcahy.

I kiss Lynn goodbye and head to the pickup area at Jessica's school. I arrive at 11:55 and she is already waiting at the curb for me. She is all smiles today and happy to get out of school early. I ask her if she thinks we should pick up some pizza for lunch, and looking at the expression on her face, she is all in. We will stop at Al's pizza and pick up two large pepperoni pizzas with extra cheese, just the way Mom likes it, although my cardiologist would ground me if he ever knew of my recent eating habits. Whatever, this is a special day and I want everyone to be comfortable when we prepare for our meeting.

On the way there, I discussed with Jessica how we are planning to proceed with Dr. Mulcahy. Suddenly, her enthusiasm over picking up pizza turns into a horror show. Once I started discussing the meeting as just casual conversation, Jessica erased her smile, looked at her shoes like she always does when she gets anxious, folded her arms, and began rocking back and forth in the passenger seat of our SUV. I am stunned. I really don't know what I could have said or done to make her react this way.

We arrive at Al's House of Pizza, and I take Jessica inside the parlor with me. We pick up the pizzas, then she marches right back to the SUV doing the same thing, rocking back and forth with her arms folded. There is no rhyme or reason for this behavior. I am clueless why she is acting this way. I thought she would want to discuss the meeting because she wanted to be there. This is why we got permission to have her attend it with us.

When we arrive back at the townhouse with the pizzas in our hand, Jessica walks around me and marches straight into her room without saying a word. Lynn asks "What's up with Jessica? What did you say to her?" I respond, "I said nothing out of the ordinary except we were going to meet all together with Dr. Mulcahy on Tuesday. Then she started acting all weird." Lynn responds, "I don't know what you mean by weird Josh. She is just a child. Give her some space."

I told Lynn I didn't know what she was even talking about when she commented on Jessica's behavior. Lynn responds, "This is my point, Josh. You are so oblivious of everything going on around you that your own child's ability to reach you when acting out is strange to you because you just don't get it!"

I am way out in left field at this time because I am falling victim to my daughter's behavior, which I don't understand. "Lynn, tell me what I am doing wrong with Jessica? Why are you guys ganging up on me?" Lynn responds, "There you go again Josh. You are being the victim once again. You are at the center of your universe, and nothing else exists. You justify all your actions by playing your 'get out of jail free card.' You always look to land on your feet, even when the floor falls below them. When will this end?"

Quietly, Jessica comes out of her room and sits on my lap and smiles. She has a huge grin on her face as she grabs my hand and puts her head on my shoulders. She doesn't even look at her mother, who remains silent. It seems that Lynn believes that Jessica will say the right things to me and make me feel better, which Lynn can't at the moment. Jessica, holding my hand, smiling at me, and putting her head on my shoulder, makes me feel comforted for some reason that I can't explain.

Jessica, after a moment of pause, lifts her head from my shoulder and quietly says, "Daddy, I have autism. The doctor at school explained it to me. She said she told you and Mommy about it. She said they will be testing me to decide what to do about it." I look at her, realizing in this moment that we are all in this same boat together with our challenges. I ask her the following question: "Jessica, do you know what autism is?" She responds, "Yes I do, Daddy. My doctor explained it to me. She said that I am very smart but act weird sometimes. She asked me if I can control it when I get weird." Lynn looks over at me and flips her hands in the air, as if to say she doesn't have a clue how to address this conversation I am having with our daughter.

"Jessica, weird is just a term that is used when someone is acting out of the ordinary." She immediately chimes in, "Daddy, when you get angry and you fold your arms and sometimes get very angry and stamp your feet, do you think that is weird? Daddy, when Mommy says something that you don't like, when you are having a fight with her, sometimes do you try to talk louder than she does so you can't hear her voice anymore? Is this what you're talking about when you say weird?" Before I can get the next word out, Jessica goes on to the next sentence. "When you refuse to talk to Mommy; when she says something you don't like; when you fold your arms, go upstairs into your office and slam the door... is that weird?"

I really don't know how to answer Jessica right now, as she is right. She goes on to say, "Daddy, just because I am smart doesn't mean that I don't feel the same things everybody else does. If I wasn't so smart, they wouldn't be testing me for autism. They would just say that I was a brat and send me for correction training or to the principal's office for discipline." I look at her in such amazement, at her assessment of the situation, but also realize how much emotional intelligence she does have on top of her very high IQ.

I ask Jessica to hang around for my meeting with her mother, about what we are going to say to Dr. Mulcahy. Her response is "Daddy, I have a lot of homework to do. You have grown up stuff to do. I am OK with that."

Lynn and I continue our discussion, and map out the details of what we are going to say to Dr. Mulcahy on Tuesday, October 25th, when our collective fates as a family will be discussed. At this point, the discussion will lead to the future of Differencia, to talk about the future leadership team that will lead this company in the 21st century.

Lessons Learned

Lynn and Jessica poke fun at Josh for coming down to breakfast with non-matching socks.

Josh reflects that when he was working full time, he neglected his family relationships.

Josh returns to household duties and does not think about job-related concerns.

Lynn returns from driving Jessica to school and she and Josh discuss the upcoming meeting with Dr. Mulcahy and their future at Differencia.

Josh recognizes that he, Lynn and Jessica will remain financially solvent for the rest of their lives.

Lynn receives a call from Jessica's school.

Gifted children at Jessica's school are assessed periodically for any changes in their learning patterns and behavior.

Lynn receives a phone call from Dr. Minerva Jones from the Putt Institute for Gifted Children. She extends the phone to Josh. He responds in disdain to Dr. Jones about not recognizing his status as Jessica's father.

Dr. Jones tells Josh that she is merely adhering to HIPAA laws regarding patient confidentiality.

Dr. Jones indicates to Josh and Lynn that Jessica has been exhibiting abnormal behavior at school. She asserts that Jessica may be autistic and wants to perform a series of tests.

Very gifted children with high IQ's can be autistic.

Lynn and Dr. Jones agree that Jessica should remain in school during her evaluation period. Lynn and Josh agree to schedule an appointment with Dr. Jones to discuss Jessica's condition. Lynn and Josh discuss their upcoming meeting with Dr. Mulcahy and next steps in their collective futures at Differencia.

Lynn tells Josh that they both are facing life-threatening conditions that must seriously be connected going forward.

Josh asserts that he is ready to face the future. Lynn tells Josh that he has personal and professional boundaries that need to be recognized.

Lynn lashes out at Josh and indicates that he is only thinking about himself. Josh responds that he is doing his best to be a good provider, a good father, and a decent CEO to Differencia. She tells him that he is neglecting her and Jessica in pursuing his professional life.

Josh muses that he and Lynn picked up the pieces at Medical Solutions and started a new company called Differencia. In doing this, he put his professional ego ahead of family. He apologizes to Lynn for doing this and says he must now modify his behavior.

Josh picks Jessica up at school and they pick up pizza on their way home. He notices that Jessica is uneasy and is rocking back and forth, as when she is under stress. He is confused by this.

Lynn asks Josh what is bothering Jessica. He responds by saying that they only discussed the upcoming meeting with Dr. Mulcahy. Lynn reprimands him for being oblivious to his surrounding environment.

Josh laments he's constantly being criticized for circumstances beyond his control. Lynn then responds that Josh is again exhibiting the victim mentality.

Jessica tells Josh that she understands that she has autism, and because of this she sometimes acts "weird." She mentions that she sometimes acts weird when he and Lynn have an argument.

Josh marvels at Jessica's EQ (emotional intelligence).

Jessica says that she need not participate in the discussion of the meeting with Dr. Mulcahy.

Lynn and Josh discuss the upcoming meeting with Dr. Mulcahy.

Questions to Ponder

Do you believe that when Josh was working full time, he neglected his family relationships? Have you neglected your family relationships in pursuing your career objectives?

Does Jessica's autism mask her IQ? Many autistic individuals are very intelligent. Have you ever worked with someone who is autistic? If so, how did you treat them? Did you listen to them, or did you dismiss their thoughts? Did they exhibit any unusual mannerisms? How could you have treated them better?

Is Josh's response to Dr. Jones's phone call about Jessica's condition reasonable? If not, how should he have reacted?

Was Dr. Jones's reaction to Josh's outburst effective? Would you have reacted differently? If so, what would you have done?

Is Dr. Jones's description of the behavior of autistic individuals clear? Could it be improved? If so, how?

Is Lynn's criticism of Josh for only thinking of his career realistic? If not, why not? Have you confronted a significant other for similar behavior? Would you react differently today based upon Josh's reaction?

Is Josh's reaction to Jessica's behavior realistic?

Should Jessica be allowed to be present in school during the evaluation?

Can Josh's victim mentality be changed? If so, how?

Key Leadership Qualities Identified

Recognizing Autism - Identifying in others bizarre behavior, such as incoherent outbursts. This often leads to antagonism of others and damages relationships.

Tolerance - Accepting unconventional behavior and responding in a positive manner. It tends to increase trust between individuals.

Bulldog Mentality - Overcoming the victimized outlook. Recognizing that one's fate is molded by proactive, not reactive behavior.

Work Life Balance - Realizing that life success results from achieving an optimal balance between one's personal and professional lives. It requires careful planning on a day-to-day basis.

Accepting Imperfections - Recognizing that perfection is a journey, not a destination. Strive to become better with each passing day.

Chapter 8
The Challenges of Succession

The day has finally arrived. It is Tuesday, October 25th, 2022. It is 9:00 AM sharp. It is a beautiful, sunny day, and we are sitting with Dr. Mulcahy, chair of the Board of Directors of Differencia. We are all seated at her conference table in total silence. I feel nauseous, and the room is spinning. My hands are cold and clammy, and my lips are parched. Jessica is sitting between me and her mother. Yet, she is not fidgeting in the least. Lynn is pensively staring at the polished grooves on the conference table.

Finally, Dr. Mulcahy says, "Let's begin our discussion with a prayer, to find solutions that will impact the future of everyone in this room after we end our meeting today." Dr. Mulcahy looks at Jessica and says softly to her, "Jessica, would you like to lead us in a prayer?" Jessica is silent and puts her head down on her mother's lap. I don't know what to expect next.

Finally, Jessica lifts her head up and reaches her hands out to me and Lynn. I am feeling very strange right now, because I don't know what to expect from this child. Jessica begins her prayer. "Dear God, Mommy and Daddy are confused on leaving their job. I don't understand what they are afraid of. I saw them both almost die. But God, you made them not die. I saw a little girl die in the hospital from Covid, and a priest that did not know why you made their daughter die. Mommy was supposed to die, but you saved her. Daddy would be all alone. But he still has me, and we would need to be strong for each other."

Jessica takes a break and continues. I am watching the tears flowing from Lynn's eyes, as Dr. Mulcahy remains silent. "God, Mommy and Daddy started a new company, but need to let someone else run it while they get better. I am here because maybe someday I will be the one to run this company, because I am smart, and I come from Mommy and Daddy. We are all the company…amen!"

Dr. Mulcahy thanks Jessica. She asks Dr. Mulcahy if she can finish her homework while we meet. Dr. Mulcahy dismisses her, and we begin our meeting. Lynn opens with her thoughts and jumps right into the meeting at the starting gate. "Bonnie, we have been friends and colleagues for a long time now. We have seen Medical Solutions evolve from a scandal to a successful new company, and have successfully managed to develop a drug that can slow down and potentially cure Parkinson's disease in its early stages. We have built to date an amazing legacy for our new company, Differencia. Who knows where we can go from here."

Dr. Mulcahy thanks Lynn for her opening comments about the successes this team has had in recent years. Dr. Mulcahy is next to remark. "Lynn and Josh, there are several line items that I need to bring to the Board of Directors this Friday. As you know, as chair of the BOD, I have a fiduciary obligation to prompt a vote on an appropriate leadership model that will keep this company and its

11,000+ employees going while you guys are rehabilitating."

I chime in next. "Bonnie, as you know, I have risen through the ranks of this company, with the assistance of my wife and trusted business partner, Lynn. I couldn't have done this without her. She has mentored and taught me so many things over the years that I could never have learned without her able assistance." Bonnie smiled at me and prompted me to continue. "As you know, my medical condition has prompted me to take some serious time off from work. Yet, I was determined to return to my job once I rehabilitated from my cardiac problem. I must admit that Lynn and I have disagreed about my returning to the job anytime soon, or in the foreseeable future." Bonnie continues to listen intently, and once again prompts me to continue. "After much deliberation, and I must confess, heated discussion, Lynn and I have decided that for the foreseeable future and perhaps beyond, it is not advisable or in the best interests of Differencia and its employees, for us to return to work as Co-CEO's. Because of my medical condition, my cardiologist recommended that I keep my stress levels low, as to avoid another attack of ventricular fibrillation, which could prove fatal."

Bonnie folds her hands neatly on the heavily polished mahogany table in her office and takes a deep breath, followed by a long sigh. She then looks at me and Lynn. Her face reddens to the color of a ripened tomato, and tears begin to flow from her eyes. I don't believe I have ever seen her in such an emotional state. Lynn reaches out to her and asks, "Bonnie, what is going on? Are you OK? It's alright. We will get through this together. Tell me what's wrong!"

Dr. Mulcahy gains her composure and says, "I have Multiple Sclerosis." I just found out last week when the test results came in. I am in the early stages, but have an aggressive form of the disease. As you know, MS affects the brain, spinal cord, and central nervous system. I started noticing changes in my balance when getting up and down from my seat at work, and in and out of my car. My eye and hand coordination were not in sync. Then, I was dropping things out of my hand for no reason. Then I noticed I couldn't focus well when reading."

Lynn responds to Bonnie very sympathetically. "Bonnie, I am so very sorry to hear this news. How are you going to handle this with the BOD?" Bonnie looks at Lynn and takes another deep breath. Her hands are still folded on the conference table in her office. "Lynn, I need to resign my position with the Board."

Lynn bounces back with a stern message to her. "Bonnie, you are one of the architects of Differencia. You saved my reputation, Josh's reputation, through thick and thin. You brought us through a major scandal and kept this company going while we were scrambling to find answers to stay on top of things. You showed true leadership in the face of adversity."

Dr. Mulcahy responds. "Lynn, all of this may be true. However, I can no longer remain in my present capacity with this disease. I also get tired more often now. Some days, my energy levels are very low. This doesn't get better Lynn. You can only treat it to ease some of the pain and stiffness that accompany the disease. I am a medical doctor. I know what is coming, Lynn."

Now it is my turn to respond. "Bonnie, Lynn and I have been to hell and back. We have all made mistakes along the way, trying to solve major problems in this company, that included some serious scandals. Yet, we survived it all and turned the page. We can't just let all of this go right now. We must find a way to keep going, to persevere through the storm. I remember that one of my professors in grad school once told us, in sociology class, that life is a marathon and not a sprint. This always stuck with me."

Lynn chimes in. "OK, so here we are, a top leadership trio of physical misfits, trying to climb Mt. Everest. We cannot see our way of getting to the top of the mountain, because we are not physically able to overcome the weather-related obstacles that stand in our way. Well, what do true leaders do? Do they give up on the climb? No, they do not. They find alternative ways to get to the top, facing the obstacles by thinking through the process, focusing only on the goals and not the obstacles."

Bonnie rebounds. "What are you trying to say to me, Lynn? We are not climbing Mt. Everest. We are trying to keep a twenty-billion-dollar company going, with eleven thousand employees researching ways to keep people alive. Where is this discussion going?"

Now it is my turn. "Bonnie, I have been the biggest screw up in the history of this company, and perhaps every company I've worked for since I got out of college. Here I am today, talking to the director of the BOD of a twenty-billion-dollar company, as one of the company's CEO's. My entire life was focused on giving allegiance to myself, and sucking all the resources out of everyone who helped me along the way, just so I would always land on my feet."

Lynn puts her hand up and tells me to let it go. "It's OK now. We need to move on." I don't agree and keep going. Lynn remains silent, and Bonnie just stares at me continuing to look at her folded hands on the conference table.

"Bonnie, I agree with Lynn that we need to think about the greater good here. We cannot allow the Board of Directors to lose confidence in our leadership despite our physical, mental, and emotional maladies. These are the obstacles that Lynn was talking about when telling her story about Mt. Everest. Lynn is right. It's the climb, not the obstacles in the way, that get us to the goal. We need to know how to climb better and overcome obstacles. We can't give up on ourselves."

Lynn observes Bonnie's facial expression, and excuses herself to check up on Jessica. Bonnie and I are alone in her office, and the mood is quite awkward and downright somber. We sat in silence for about thirty seconds when Lynn steps back into the meeting. She tells us that Jessica is getting bored and wants to know if she can use the scratchpad in Bonnie's office to do some drawing. Bonnie gives her the scratchpad with a big smile and Jessica once again leaves the office to sit in the atrium.

Lynn is somber and quite fidgety, and Dr. Mulcahy appears to want to say something to both of us that we need to hear. Lynn, for no reason, stares at Bonnie, and you could feel the tension mounting between the two of them. I can't figure out this intuitive disarray and tension that is going on, between the two most important people in my circle besides Jessica.

Finally, Lynn fires up the muster to say something I never thought I would hear coming out of her. "Bonnie, how could you not say anything to us when you first started feeling the symptoms of your disease? How could you wait over a week to tell us what was going on with you, when you knew we were coming in today to basically resign from our positions for the greater good of Differencia? Bonnie, why did you let it get to this point, on this day to drop this on us?"

Bonnie does not answer Lynn. Rather she directs her motions in my direction. "Josh, how long did it take you to tell anyone at Medical Solutions that Lynn was missing, and you were going to make a breakthrough medical announcement with her? What kept you from telling Dr. Fringe, who was the BOD director at that time?"

I have never seen this side of Bonnie Mulcahy. She is trying to justify not telling us about her MS by trading "an eye for an eye" scenario, to justify her reasons for not telling us she was sick. I respond to her this way. "Bonnie, I was wrong by not letting the company know what was going on. Could I justify not saying anything about Lynn missing, landing in the hospital? Of course, I could justify my actions because I am human. My mind was cluttered with what I should do next. How do I address this with my daughter? How can I explain it to her if her mother doesn't make it?"

At this point, Lynn tries to chime in and take over the conversation. I put up my hand to continue my response to Dr. Mulcahy when Jessica comes into the office to return the scratch pad she borrowed. She walks over to Dr. Mulcahy and hands her the scratch pad, with a drawing and a message beneath the drawing. Bonnie's face reddens once again, and the tears flow freely from her tear ducts onto her green, silk blouse.

Lynn looks over to Bonnie and asks her if she is all right. Dr. Mulcahy turns the scratchpad in the direction of me and Lynn. Both of us are blown away at what we are looking at. It is a drawing of the little girl Jessica watched die in the hospital from Covid. Beneath the drawing, she wrote: "Stop fighting and stop thinking of yourselves. Be leaders even when you are sick. She did not have to die."

Jessica asked if she could leave and go outside the office once again. I put my hand up and asked Jessica to take a seat. I wanted her to hear what I was about to say. "Bonnie, me, Lynn and Jessica, our family supports everything Differencia stands for. We have put our hearts and souls into this company, both personally and professionally. We want you to know that we have learned so much from each other and our experiences both inside and outside this operation. We have weathered storms, through thick and thin. We want to consider you a part of our family."

Bonnie responds with gratitude and admiration for our family, and how we feel about her being a member of our family. Over the next several months, we will develop and present to the Board of Directors a solid, strategic plan for Differencia. Bonnie Mulcahy will resign as the chair of the BOD, and immediately ask for a full vote among the board members, to elect a new chair at the meeting on Friday, October 28, 2022.

Dr. Mulcahy, Chair of the Board of Directors, Dr. Lynn Ann Marconi, and Joshua Keating (Co-CEOs) of Differencia will immediately resign their positions at this meeting.

The results of the meeting, held with the Board of Directors at 10:00 AM, are recorded as follows:

1) Dr. Ingrid Frost, Board Certified Chemist and Consultant, has been chosen to replace Dr. Bonnie Mulcahy as Board Chair.

2) Dr. Lynn Ann Marconi and Joshua Keating, Co-CEOs of Differencia, will resign their positions indefinitely, until it satisfies the BOD they can return to work in their respective capacities.

3) Dr. Ingrid Frost, by unanimous consent with Board members of Differencia, will appoint a special task force reporting to the

BOD. This task force will represent the top experts in each major department of Differencia, to keep the company functional and sustainable until an extensive search, not to exceed six months, for a new CEO, has been completed and validated by said Board.

4) Both Dr. Mulcahy and Dr. Marconi will remain as voting Board Members.

5) The Board will reconvene on April 1, 2023, with all results.

Lessons Learned

Josh, Lynn and Jessica arrive in Dr. Mulcahy's office for their meeting with her.

Dr. Mulcahy asks Jessica to lead her, Josh, and Lynn in prayer.

Jessica says that she saw her mother and father almost die, and saw a little girl die in the hospital.

Jessica indicates that she, Josh, and Lynn must remain strong for each other, and that someday she may very well run Differencia.

Lynn tells Dr. Mulcahy that she and Josh were very successful in allowing Medical Solutions to overcome the past scandal.

Dr. Mulcahy indicates that several line items need to be presented to the Board, including the formation of an appropriate leadership model for the Company's 11,000 employees.

Josh asserts, after considerable discussion, that he and Lynn have decided that for the foreseeable future, it is not in the best interests of Differencia for him and Lynn to return to work as Co-CEOs.

Josh indicates that he has made past mistakes and has found ways to overcome them. He asserts that he and Lynn cannot allow the Board of Directors to lose confidence in their leadership, despite their physical, mental, and emotional maladies.

Jessica uses the scratch pad in Dr. Mulcahy's office to do some drawing.

Lynn asks Dr. Mulcahy why she did not say anything when she first started feeling symptoms of multiple sclerosis.

Dr. Mulcahy asks Josh how long it took him to tell Dr. Fringe and the Board of Directors at Medical Solutions that Lynn was missing, and that the announcement to the Food and Drug Administration announcement would be delayed.

Jessica returns to Dr. Mulcahy's office to return the scratchpad with a message beneath a drawing. The message says, "Stop fighting and stop thinking of yourselves."

Josh tells Dr. Mulcahy that she, Lynn, and Jessica consider her a part of their family.

Dr. Mulcahy begins to cry, and Lynn asks her what is bothering her.

Dr. Mulcahy responds that she has learned that she has an aggressive form of multiple sclerosis, which is affecting her brain, spinal cord, and central nervous system.

Lynn asks her how she is going to inform the Board of Directors of her medical condition. Dr. Mulcahy indicates that she needs to resign her position with the Board.

Lynn praises her for being one of the architects of Differencia, and that she has shown true leadership in the face of adversity.

Josh muses that he, Lynn, and Dr. Mulcahy have all faced obstacles in the past and found ways to overcome them, in the achievement of their goals.

Lynn indicates that she, Josh, and Dr. Mulcahy must seek alternative ways to overcome the challenges of Mount Everest.

Dr. Mulcahy indicates that they are not climbing Mount Everest, but are seeking to lead a $20 billion company with over 11,000 employees.

Dr. Mulcahy responds with gratitude, and indicates that over the next several months, Differencia will develop and present to the Board of Directors a strategic plan for Differencia going forward. She will resign as Chair of the Board of Directors, and ask for a full vote announcing the decision to elect a new Board Chair.

Josh and Lynn will resign their positions indefinitely, until they can return to work in their respective capacities.

Dr. Frost will appoint a special task force to keep Differencia functioning, until a new CEO is appointed.

Dr. Mulcahy and Lynn will remain as voting Board members.

Questions to Ponder

Do you agree with Dr. Mulcahy's decision to ask Jessica to open the meeting with a prayer? Why or why not? Do you think that this will lead to a more productive meeting?

Do you open your business meetings with a prayer?

Do you have members of your inner circle who are autistic? How do you solicit their opinions? What are the advantages of doing this?

Is Josh and Lynn's decision to take an indefinite leave of absence before turning to work reasonable? What would you have done if you were faced with similar circumstances?

Is Dr. Mulcahy justified in delaying the announcement of her multiple sclerosis condition? What would you have done?

Is Dr. Mulcahy's retort to Josh, that he did a similar thing in informing company employees of Lynn's condition only after considerable time had elapsed, valid?

Do you agree with Jessica's claim that Josh and Lynn are only thinking of themselves, and not their professional and personal lives?

Is Josh telling Dr. Mulcahy that she is part of the family a productive approach in improving her mindset? Have you used a similar approach in a past situation you were faced with?

Given Dr. Mulcahy's MS diagnosis, is her decision to resign reasonable? Should she "tough it out?" What would you do?

Is Josh's perspective that he, Lynn and Dr. Mulcahy can overcome their current obstacles through sheer determination sound? What course of action should they take? Have you addressed similar obstacles in your past? What was the result? Would you have acted differently today?

Given the evolution of Dr. Mulcahy's character, what is your current assessment of her leadership skills?

Key Leadership Qualities Identified

Prayer - A petition to God or a higher being. A request to an external source for help. It is often a prelude to collective decision-making.

Determination - Firm resolve in the pursuit of a goal or objective. Obstacles are viewed as challenges and opportunities. It cultivates an entrepreneurial mindset.

Inner Circle - Close associates, whether personal or professional. Members of the inner circle are consulted in making decisions. Trusted advisors share similar goals and objectives.

Timely Communication - Sharing one's thoughts with others on an ad hoc basis. It builds trust by fostering transparency, moment to moment.

Understanding - Striving to understand the mindset and goals and objectives of others. It fosters the ability to influence others successfully.

Chapter 9

April 1, 2023 The New CEO

After six months of collaboration with employees, administration, consultants and pharmaceutical partners, the Board of Directors, with unanimous consent under the leadership of Dr. Ingrid Frost, Board Chair, selected Dr. Francesco Romano, Ph.D. as the next CEO of Differencia.

Dr. Romano is a board-certified chemist, whose father started Reginald Research Pharmaceuticals in Spokane, WA, not far from Seattle, in 1983, over forty years ago. Dr. Romano's Dad, William, graduated from The Massachusetts College of Pharmacy in 1963 and opened Romano Pharmacy in 1965, after moving from Newton, MA to Seattle, WA. He met his wife while she was studying for her Ph.D. in archaeology at Tufts University in Cambridge, MA. Her family was from Seattle, and he moved there to be with her.

Dr. Reginald Romano, Pharm.D., was so enthralled with pharmaceutical medicines that he sold his very successful pharmaceutical business, which had three locations in the state of Washington, to an investment group. In October, 1983, the proceeds from the sale were put into a new research venture in pharmaceuticals, and was named Reginald Research Pharmaceuticals. Dr. Romano immediately partnered with many of his colleagues of similar interests, and prompted them to invest in his new research company, naming them to the board of this newly formed capital venture. He raised over $3 million dollars in his first two years. During that time, Francesco was born to Mary (formerly Sweeney) and Reginald Romano at 6 pounds and eleven ounces, in Seattle, on November 5, 1985.

Francesco was always very quiet. However, just like his Dad, had a keen interest in pharmaceutical research, specifically in the areas of neurological and autoimmune diseases such as Parkinson's, MS and autoimmune dementia. Francesco received his undergraduate degree (A.B.) in Molecular and Cellular Biology in 1997. He then went on to receive his Ph.D. in Biochemistry and Molecular Biology in 2006. Both degrees were from regionally accredited Universities in the U.S. He was ready to work in his father's company and follow in his footsteps. He wrote several articles on autoimmune diseases, specifically dealing with Parkinson's and M.S.

In 2010, Francesco had a close friend who worked at the University of Southern California Medical school. He was so impressed with Francesco's research that he arranged a meeting with the associate dean of the school of medicine, who was specifically interested in his work in Pharmaceutical and Health Economics associated with regulatory sciences. This made sense, as this was actually a department at USC, in Pharmacology.

The dean was immediately impressed with Francesco. After four long, thorough, and grueling interviews, the dean of Pharmacology offered Francesco an assistant professor's position in Pharmaceutical and Health Economics. Francesco rose quickly through the ranks, going from Assistant Professor to Associate Professor to Professor, by 2016. In 2017, the associate dean retired, and Francesco was offered his position. In 2019, Francisco was appointed Dean of the School of Pharmacology. In the past, he had written several published, peer-reviewed articles, appearing in over 100 medical journals and magazines worldwide.

Six months ago, he started interviewing for the position of CEO at Differencia, among one hundred and twenty-five applicants. The rest is history, for the reasons mentioned above. He got the job! He appeared to be a perfect match for what Differencia was searching for in a new CEO, on so many levels.

What is to follow is the speech given to the Board of Directors at Differencia on Thursday, April 13th, 2023, at 3:00 PM, Pacific Time. All eleven thousand employees, including staff and administrative management, could stream the speech live. This was truly a historic day for Differencia.

Dear Board Members and Stakeholders of Differencia. I am humbled and proud to become a member of this wonderful establishment, following an exhaustive search to choose the right candidate to fill such an important and transformative position, at this time.

I believe that my credentials are only part of the reason why I was chosen to lead this prestigious organization that is on the verge of tremendous success with breakthrough drugs that have potential to enhance the quality of life for millions of people globally.

I believe I am also here because I embrace your new mission, to research better ways to make medicine affordable to all that need it, while at the same time covering the tremendous costs to research, experiment, and discover the right combination of natural and synthetic resources to make the most effective drugs, to cure the most aggressive and debilitating diseases.

This will not be easy. Yet, it is not impossible. In this organization, we have some of the most talented researchers on the planet. Many of them work 12, 14, 16 hours a day, hoping to improve the quality of life of individuals. Unfortunately, most can't afford these drugs, because they are too expensive to create and distribute in large quantities.

Together, we can change how we look at curing diseases, by building better research institutions that can innovate and teach young research scientists, in the fields of molecular biology and biochemistry. They can be mentored by many of the talented individuals working in this company.

My Dad has been my coach and mentor for several decades, and prompted me to follow in his footsteps. It would have been my honor and pleasure to continue working in his pharmaceutical research company, Reginal Research Pharmaceuticals. However, after receiving my Ph.D. in Biochemistry and Molecular Biology in 2006, I had a yearning to teach my craft, because I believed I could make a difference in how we research new and innovative drugs that treat diseases that affect the autoimmune system.

Since 2010, I have held several positions at the University of Southern California's Medical School, in the Department of Pharmacology. My interests were specifically in health economics and regulatory sciences. I recently left my position at USC, where I served as the Dean of The School of Pharmacology, since 2019. Here I am today, at Differencia.

My goal is to lead this company as CEO, and my vision (already discussed with this Board and one of the main reasons why I was hired) is to start a university, as a division of this company, for research and development of breakthrough autoimmune drugs that will obliterate the devastating effects of crippling and life-threatening diseases, for all that need them. Our goal, through educational research, is to develop less expensive methods to produce these drugs, while giving our shareholders a decent profit margin for their investments. Our university will be dually structured: to teach and promote innovative research methodologies for developing and distributing groundbreaking pharmaceutical drugs; and to hire the most talented and gifted applicants to work at Differencia, to fulfill our vision, mission and goals.

Together, we can accomplish these goals and make a difference. As we speak, my Dad is talking to his investors about buying into this newly revised mission for Differencia. The Board, led by Dr. Ingrid Frost, has approved this plan to go forward.

Finally, Dr. Bonnie Mulcahy, former Board Chair, Dr. Lynn Ann Marconi, and Joshua Keating will serve as consultants to start this new venture of education at Differencia. They will report to me and

Dr. Frost. Our plan is to have them play major administrative roles, and under their guidance and leadership, participate in the planning, formation, and execution of our new university, to be named in the not-too-distant future. We will be bringing you up to date as plans move forward.

I will officially begin my tenure as Differencia's new CEO on June 1, 2023. We will plan, restructure, and reassess our vision, mission and strategic leadership team going forward, for many years to follow. In the interim, Dr. Frost and I will work with her BOD, Dr. Mulcahy, Dr. Marconi, and Josh Keating, as Differencia follows its namesake: "To make a difference."

Dr. Francesco Romano, CEO-Elect, Differencia

Lessons Learned

After six months, the Board of Directors selected Dr. Francesco Romano, Ph.D. as the next CEO of Differencia.

Dr. Romano is a board-certified chemist, whose father started Reginald Research Pharmaceuticals. His father opened Romano Pharmacy in 1965.

Dr. Reginald Romano sold his successful pharmaceutical business to an investment group. He partnered with several colleagues to start a new research venture, and raised over $3 million in the first two years.

Dr. Francesco Romano was born in Seattle, Washington, in November, 1985. He had a keen interest in pharmaceutical research, in the areas of neurological and autoimmune diseases.

Francesco earned an A.B. in Molecular and Cellular Biology in 1997, and a Ph.D. in Biochemical and Molecular Biology, in 2006.

After an interview with the associate dean of Pharmacology and faculty members, Dr. Romano was offered a faculty position at the University of Southern California Medical School. He rose rapidly through the faculty ranks, and was promoted from associate dean to dean in 2019.

In the immediate years to follow, Francesco was selected as CEO of Differencia.

In his acceptance speech, Dr. Romano noted the following:

—He is humbled to be selected for such an important faculty position.

—He believed the credentials were only part of the reason that he was offered the position

—He asserts he was chosen because he embraced the mission of performing research to make medicine more affordable, and to discover the right combination of natural and synthetic resources to make the most cost-effective drugs.

—Life-saving drugs must be produced at an affordable cost.

—Better research institutions can teach young research scientists in the fields of molecular biology and biochemicals.

—It is his desire to shape the research to be performed in developing new and innovative drugs to attack diseases that affect the autoimmune system.

—His goal is to start a university as a division of Differencia, which will foster the research and development of breakthrough autoimmune drugs that will effectively attack the devastating effects of life-threatening diseases.

—The production and distribution of life-saving drugs should be consistent with providing a decent profit margin for Differencia.

—The Board, led by Dr. Frost, has approved the plan to go forward.

—Dr. Mulcahy, Dr. Marconi, and Josh Keating will serve as consultants to Differencia. Dr. Mulcahy and Dr. Marconi will report to both Francesco and Dr. Frost.

—Francesco will begin his tenure as Differencia's CEO in June, 2023.

Questions to Ponder

Given the stated mission of Differencia –to produce cost-effective and affordable life-saving drugs, does Dr. Romano's selection as CEO seem like a wise choice? Why or why not? Does his background qualify him for the position?

Was Dr. Reginald Romano's decision to sell his successful pharmaceutical business a wise one? What would you have done?

Have you ever sold a business that was successful, and used the proceeds to form a new business or businesses? If so, what was the result? Would you make the same decision today?

Do you agree with Dr. Francesco Romano's decision to accept a faculty position? Why or why not?

Was Dr. Romano's decision to accept an administrative position in the medical field a wise one? What would you have done? What are the advantages and disadvantages of doing this?

What is your assessment of Dr. Romano's acceptance speech? How could it be improved? Have you ever made a similar speech? How could you have improved it?

How important are an individual's credentials in helping the firm achieve its goals and objectives? What other factors should be considered?

How important should mission alignment between an individual and an organization be, in the candidate elected?

How important are research institutions in developing effective life-saving drugs? Are there better ways of achieving this goal?

Do you agree with the decision to start a university as a division of Differencia? Why or why not? Is Dr. Romano the best individual to accomplish this?

Is Differencia entitled to a decent profit margin as it produces life-saving drugs that attack autoimmune diseases? Why or why not?

Is making a profit consistent with the risk-reward paradigm? Would you undertake a risk if the ability to earn a profit was negligible or non-existent?

Key Leadership Qualities Identified

Strategic Plan - True leader

Outstanding Credentials - Selecting the most qualified candidate for a position, based upon their skill set. Successful leaders often have an excellent skill set.

Business Divestiture - The sale of a business to finance the purchase of another business This is often necessary to achieve a newly found objective or objectives. In the fast-food industry, this led to many startups being formed.

Mission Alignment - The congruence of an individual's mission and the mission of an organization. This is crucial in that actions of the individual are consistent with both the individual's and organization's goals.

Career Flexibility - Willingness to change one's career to achieve a new goal or objective. Abraham Lincoln shifted from being a lawyer to pursuing a career in politics, so as to preserve the union.

Transformational Leadership - Increasing focus in an organization, in order to develop a pathfinding strategy to accomplish important goals and objectives. Martin Luther King Jr. placed strong focus on non-violence as the primary way to promote the goals of the civil rights movement.

Risk-Reward Paradigm - The belief that reward is proportional to the risk undertaken. Bill Gates' development of Microsoft was the result of a huge investment that was successful. Disney's success in the field of animation is another excellent example.

Chapter 10

Francesco Romano, The New CEO, Begins His Tenure

At 10:00 AM, June 1, 2023, Differencia's Board of Directors meeting was formally opened by Dr. Ingrid Frost, the Board Chair, who announced that the BOD at Differencia would be handing full organizational responsibilities over to its new CEO, Dr. Francesco Romano, Ph.D. The announcement was made, ensuring the Board's pledge and commitment to Dr. Romano, to take Differencia to a new plateau of successful ventures, in providing affordable drugs to those suffering from debilitating diseases. The pledge included providing the resources needed to manufacture these drugs.

Among the resources, it was quite apparent and made quite clear six months earlier by Dr. Romano, that a new university would be created as part of Differencia's new venture, to make drugs that could cure debilitating diseases, and make them affordable for all those who needed them to maintain a suitable quality of life.

Dr. Romano would begin this venture by meeting with the investors who bought his Dad's company, Reginald Research Pharmaceuticals. The company had expanded to ten locations, and was involved in extensive research for drugs to help cure neurological and pulmonary diseases. Although his Dad had retired, he convinced the investors that bought his company that Differencia's ambition, through his son's efforts to open a university, would also help them expand their efforts to be successful while making them quite profitable in the process, and be a definite plus for their research efforts.

Romano stated, "I realized that leadership often involves looking at the reality of profitable enterprise, while also serving the corporate commitment of social responsibility that serves the greater good." In essence, Reginald Research Pharmaceuticals would be able to strategically partner with Differencia, to educate the best research scientists to produce many drugs in large volumes that could help cure and perhaps eradicate some of the most debilitating diseases on the planet.

After several meetings with Differencia's Board of Directors, Dr. Francesco Romano, Reginald Romano, and his investor group (Parent Company Diamond Medical Research Group), decided to donate $300 million dollars to break ground on the new university.

Joshua Keating (yes, that is me, the voice of this narrative) has been assigned as the project manager of this new enterprise. "I am honored to be a part of this new venture. As the new PM, I will be responsible for working with every resource available, financially and materialistically, to develop this into a growing educational establishment. I will be responsible for working with all vendors, consultants, internal resources, investors, and all stakeholders. I have been given a timeline of three years to get this project off the ground and running. The university will be built on a 400-acre plot of land that has been donated by the investor group as part of their $300 million dollar investment."

The BOD has also decided to name Dr. Bonnie Mulcahy the chief consultant in charge of choosing trustees, and administratively staffing this new university, as the project is being built. She will have the autonomy to choose trustees for this new university. However, she, nor any member of the BOD at Differencia including their CEO, can serve as a trustee. This would be a conflict of interests and would appear discriminatory to decisions made between the university and the company. Although one is a part of the other, their objectives will be kept separate for legal and ethical reasons.

It is June 7th, 2023, and Lynn gets a call from her sister Mary. They have a very nice conversation on the phone, lasting almost an hour. Suddenly, I hear a loud scream coming from Lynn, and I thought something had happened to her sister. Jessica was doing her homework and comes rushing to her mother's side, saying "Mommy, are you all right?" Lynn looks at her and chuckles loudly. She sits Jessica on her lap and says to her, "Go get Daddy, hurry up!"

Jessica runs into my office, as I am beginning to plan my next venture as the project manager of a new university. I have a million phone calls to make before I even get started, and I hesitate to leave my office. Lynn shouts to Jessica once again, "Go get Daddy, hurry!" Jessica responds to her, "I'm with him, Mommy, and he won't come downstairs. He is busy and writing down a lot of things on his scratchpad. I hear Lynn run up the stairs and trip briefly along the way, before she enters my office. She is out of breath and tells me to pick up the phone and put it in speaker mode.

Lynn, still out of breath, speaks with her sister. "Mary, are you still there?" She responds, "Yes, Lynn, I am here. Are you with Josh and Jessica right now?" Lynn responds affirmatively. "I have two things to tell all three of you. I want you to listen to me carefully, because all of this may take some time to process." I respond, "OK" as Mary continues. "The first item is that after 27 years as Director of Operations of Comwide International Corporation, a $60 billion international telecommunications company specializing in social media, 200 news feeds worldwide, among many other things, I have decided to retire my position."

She continues. "As you guys may remember, I contacted you on June 6, 2022 – yes, I write everything down that I do. It is part of my job – to inform you that I was diagnosed with Parkinson's disease. Although I am doing OK, I get tired easily, and my ability to handle almost 100 direct reports and six continents around the globe is too overwhelming. I also get a lot of stiffness in my joints. Sometimes my ability to concentrate like I used to is compromised."

The mood is very somber in my office as Mary continues. "Over the years, I have saved a substantial amount of money. I never have married, and I always put my best efforts into my work. This company was my family and always treated me well. For the past 15 years, I have made a better than six-figure salary, and purchased a fair amount of stock in the company. Some of it I rolled into a 401(k) plan. I decided to put the remainder into a worthwhile investment. I decided to put it into Differencia's new university. The amount is $2.3 million."

Lynn looks at me and says, "Now you know why I was just screaming. My sister and I think very much alike, about putting money into worthwhile causes. Mary responds, "Don't get too carried away, Lynn. I have Parkinson's disease and I am looking for a cure as much as the next person who has contracted this debilitating monster that keeps us from living a normal life. I am 47 years old, and I want to have a future. I am not retiring from life. I am retiring from my present position."

After acknowledging that we understand where Mary is coming from, it all makes sense. Mary tells us the second part of her message. "I sat down with my Board of Directors when I decided to resign my position, and told them about my investment in your company. They were exhilarated to learn how much my investment into Differencia's new university meant to me, and they decided to also invest in the University as a strategic partner, with the sum of $60 million dollars. They told me that they were saddened to lose me, and that Parkinson's disease needs to be cured, or at least slowed down in its early stages, to prevent individuals like me from having to give up their jobs. I contacted your Board, and they were most happy to accept my donation and my former company's intention to strategically partner with you to build the new university."

I respond to Mary, "This is great news! I am going to be the project manager for the new university. What role will you be playing, considering your investment and influence on investors in your former company to strategically partner with Differencia?" Mary pauses for a moment and responds. "You are very perceptive, Josh. I was asked to serve as a member of your board of trustees for the new university."

Lynn was excited to hear this news and asked her sister if she accepted. Mary's response was, "Of course. It would be my pleasure and honor to be a part of this wonderful venture, especially where I am directly affected by the outcome of the research from the great scientists who will be championing this cause."

On that note, we said goodbye to Mary and just looked at each other for a moment. Lynn's response was "Go figure: what goes around, comes around in due time. This shows you how we are all connected to one another personally and professionally. Let's get ready for the new CEO to make his announcement tomorrow about the University."

It is Thursday, June 8th, 2023, and Dr. Francesco Romano will soon be announcing the new plans regarding the university. He will oversee its development over the next three years, and I will report its progress directly to him. Yes, Dr. Romano will be my new boss. I must admit, this is a lot different than being the CEO, with employees reporting to me. However, in the stream of life, as project manager overseeing a $360 million dollar operation with multiple responsibilities, in contrast, is far less stressful for my wheelhouse.

OK. It's 10:00 AM Pacific Time, and Dr. Romano is ready to start making his announcements. He will be live streaming as before, with all of Differencia's 11,000 employees on the feed. He will be appearing with the Board of Directors behind him, as he takes center stage in the auditorium of the Grand Room at Differencia, which houses about 500 members of the company's top administrators.

Good morning, ladies and gentlemen of Differencia. Today, I begin my tenure in leading this great organization, which will build the best pharmaceuticals for curing debilitating diseases that this planet has ever seen.

We are an amazing organization that has grown tremendously over the past three decades, from very humble beginnings to where it is today. When this company first took root as Medical Solutions, Inc. it had only thirty employees in a small, dilapidated warehouse, just outside of Los Angeles. It started with a few research scientists that dreamed about making drugs that could help doctors better treat their patients, so they could live longer lives.

The company grew and grew, until the unfortunate consequences of corporate creed engulfed the minds and souls of a few of our greatest scientists, who did many wonderful things for this company. They were dealt with swiftly and harshly, paying the price for their misdeeds.

However, the discoveries made by Medical Solutions still provided a paradigm of skillsets, to further develop the wonder drugs only this company was able to do, in record time.

We are on the verge of putting out a drug which has the potential to cure Parkinson's Disease in its early stages, and slow the progression of the disease substantially in the moderate stages. The drug is presently going through testing at the FDA, and they will send us their preliminary results and data by June 1, 2024.

Despite an initial patent approval by the FDA in 2023, and perhaps final approval by the end of 2024 if all testing goes well, most eligible patients for these drugs may not be able to afford them, because of the costs to manufacture and distribute. Therefore, our only option is to find ways to develop the right combinations of natural and already developed synthetic resources to manufacture pharmaceuticals in large supply, so that they will be readily available to sick patients that have a chance to live with, and even get cured from, debilitating diseases such as MS and Parkinson's.

Together, we can do this by building a college dedicated to the research and further development of what we have already accomplished to date, in the potential manufacturing of pharmaceuticals that can cure MS and Parkinson's to begin with, at an affordable price for all that need it. We need to recruit the most talented individuals from colleges that specialize in our type of research, and have their eye on transformational medicine that will revolutionize our industry.

Here is the exciting news. We are drawing up the plans for the new college, and will announce them on September 1, 2023. We have hired the best surveyors and engineers in the state of California, to draw the specs for the new University. We have initial endowment pledges of $300 million dollars from The Diamond Medical Research Group, inclusive of a four-hundred-acre plot of land where the university will be built. Comwide International Corporation has also donated $60 million dollars to the establishment of the new university. The project will take three years to complete.

The project manager in charge of the operation, as well as serving as the Chief Operations Officer, will be Joshua Keating, former CEO of Differencia. Dr. Bonnie Mulcahy, former chief research scientist and Director of the BOD at Differencia, has been named as the chief consultant in charge of choosing trustees and administratively staffing this new university, as the project is developed. Dr. Lynn Ann Marconi, former CEO of Differencia, former BOD chair and member, has been chosen as the first tenured president (as chosen by the BOD) of the new university, which has been named "The Diamond College of Pharmaceutical Research."

I want to thank Dr. Ingrid Frost, Distinguished Members of the BOD of Differencia, and its 11,000 employees around the globe, for making this new venture possible. From here it is all up to us.

The End

Lessons Learned

The Differencia Board of Directors meeting has been opened by Dr. Ingrid Frost. She announces that full organizational responsibilities will be handled by the new CEO, Dr. Francesco Romano

Dr. Romano continues his commitment to establish a new university, which will provide life-saving drugs which will enhance quality of life at an affordable cost.

Dr. Romano meets with investors who bought his Dad's company, Regional Research Pharmaceuticals. He convinces them that the establishment of the university is the best approach to stimulate research in the development of these life-saving drugs.

Leadership often involves viewing the reality of a profitable business while serving true corporate commitment to social responsibility.

Dr. Romano and his investor group decide to contribute $300 million to break ground for the new university.

Joshua Keating is assigned to be project manager of the new enterprise. He is given a timeline of three years to launch and see the project though.

Dr. Bonnie Mulcahy is appointed as the chief consultant. She will choose trustees for the new university.

Lynn receives a phone call from her sister Mary, who does not react very favorably to what Mary is saying.

Lynn enters Josh's office and tells him to pick up the phone.

Mary tells Josh, Lynn, and Jessica that (1) after 27 years as Director of Operations of Comcade International Corporation, she has decided to retire from her position. (2) her Parkinson's disease is causing her increased stiffness, and her ability to concentrate is being compromised.

Mary indicates that she has decided to transfer $2.3 million of stock from her earnings at Comcade international into the new university. She indicates that she is searching for a cure for Parkinson's, which will improve afflicted individuals' quality of life. In following Mary's lead, the Board of Directors decide to invest $60 million in Differencia' s new university.

Mary accepts an invitation to serve as a member of Differencia's Board of Trustees

Dr. Francesco Romano is Josh Keating's new boss, and Josh will be responsible for overseeing the $360 million operation.

Dr. Romano states his intention to lead Differencia to become the best pharmaceutical company for curing debilitating diseases.

After Medical Solutions was restructured in response to corporate scandals, Differencia inherited a collection of skill sets to develop wonder drugs in record time.

Because of the FDA approval process for Parkinson's drugs, most eligible patients may not be able to afford them, because of their exorbitant cost. Therefore, ways must be found to develop the right combination of natural and already developed synthetic resources to manufacture pharmaceuticals in large supply, in order to cure and provide access for patients to procure MS and Parkinson's drugs at an affordable cost.

The new college needs to recruit the most talented individuals that specialize in transformational medicine.

The $300 million from the Diamond Medical Group will be used to purchase a 400-acre plot of land where the university will be built. This entire project will take three years to complete.

Josh Keating will be the Chief Operations Officer.

Dr. Bonnie Mulcahy is named the chief consultant in choosing trustees and staffing the new university.

Dr. Lynn Marconi is chosen as the first tenured president.

Questions to Ponder

Does Dr. Romano have the capability to guarantee the manufacture of life-saving drugs at an affordable cost?

Dr. Romano chooses the establishment of a university as a principal means of addressing his objective: to create lifesaving drugs at an affordable cost. Do you see any other ways he could accomplish this objective?

Meeting with angel investors is often pursued to gather funds for new enterprises. Have you ever attempted to raise funds in this way, to finance a project? What was the result? What would you do differently today?

Do authentic leaders have corporate social responsibility? How can they reconcile this with the need to maximize shareholder value? In your career, how have you handled this trade off? What are the key elements that need to be included in corporate social responsibility?

Given Josh Keating's track record as an executive, do you think he has the capability to be successful as project manager for the development of the new university?

Is the decision to hire Dr. Bonnie Mulcahy as chief consultant a wise one? Would an individual with direct fundraising experience have been a better choice? Considering your background, have you ever been faced with a similar decision? How did you handle it?

Is Mary's decision to resign her position at Comcade after 27 years as Director of Operations a good one, or should she have waited to see how her Parkinson's condition develops?

Have you ever been faced with a similar decision? How did you react? Would you have reacted differently today?

Is Mary taking on too much risk, investing $2.3 million in the new university project? Have you ever been faced with a similar situation? How did you react?

Should corporations invest funds in organizations to pursue causes that will be beneficial to a significant number of their employees? Why or why not?

Is Mary's decision to join Differencia's Board of Trustees a wise one, or should she wait to see how her medical condition develops?

Is the FDA's drug approval process too drawn out? Should it be shortened if the potential benefits far outweigh the risks?

What responsibility do pharmaceutical companies have to produce lifesaving and pain reducing drugs at an affordable cost?

Key Leadership Qualities Identified

Angel Investor - One who acts or supports with money or influence. Many startups require extensive resources to grow their enterprise. Broadway plays were often financed in this way in the early 20th century.

Corporate Social Responsibility - Environmental responsibility, ethical responsibility, philanthropic responsibility, and economic responsibility. Promoting shareholder value growth while achieving environmental, ethical, and philanthropic responsibility.

Synthetic Resources - Substances that are not produced by nature, but rather are made by humans using natural material. They include synthetic fiber, chemicals, artificial foods, and medicines. They are renewable and promote sustainability.

Appropriate Skillset - Skills which support a specific area of competence. The knowledge, experience, and abilities to do a job. They may include computer skills, communication, time management, research, planning, and leadership.

Milestones - A significant point in development. A means of tracking the progress of a project. It often signifies if more resources are needed for goal achievement.

Epilogue

From the dawn of humanity's existence, an instinct to survive has permeated the human brain in many ways, ranging from extremism: resulting in territorial domination, to collective collaboration of survival techniques: servicing the many rather than the few. In short, we referred to this perceptual regulatory process existing between both extremes as leadership.

Whether intentions to survive result in domination or collaboration, centuries of discovery have not yet determined if leadership is an innate trait of a human being, a learned response, or a combination of the two. Behavior that influences motivation in individuals, and gets them to act on foreseen and unforeseen circumstances, is commonly referred to as leadership.

Many of us who identify as leaders have either observed or practiced certain techniques that influence and motivate the behavior of others to act. Whether they act in a negative or positive way, in what society deems as helpful or harmful, these so-called leaders influence the behavior of those they lead.

Authentic leadership is not judgmental but rather, it is driven by making good judgements on difficult decisions. Ethical behavior and strong core values influence authentic leadership. However, it is about making choices to do what benefits the many.

The Verdict is the culmination of a three-book trilogy, beginning with *The Authentic Leader,* then *Differencia,* and finally *The Verdict.*

The Verdict focuses its plot on two very capable leaders (Joshua Keating and Dr. Lynn Ann Marconi) who found each other in the human connection, and evolved into Co-CEOs of "Differencia." Physical, emotional, and personal challenges sideline these leaders from their top company jobs, leaving Differencia without a CEO.

The Board of Directors must conduct an immediate and extensive search for a new CEO at Differencia, fulfilling its company vision, mission, and strategic plan. They must choose a CEO whose core values align with theirs. Time is of the essence.

After a six-month, exhaustive search, a new CEO has been chosen, with an agenda to be in line with what the company, as well as humanity, need to make a difference in how medicine can cure the most debilitating diseases. Is Differencia up to the Challenge? Is the new CEO up to the challenge?

The challenge lies in the individuals, who believe in the core values of modern medicine, the sanctity of the Hippocratic Oath, and the dignity of The Good Samaritan to make the sick well again. We need to research, learn, and develop people, as well as medicine, to make all this happen. The only answer is education.

The authors of the trilogy of books mentioned here recommend that you take the journey throughout the book series with the two main characters, Joshua Keating and Lynn Ann Marconi. Learn how other characters have evolved throughout the series as well. Get involved in the scandals and the triumphs on how Medical Solutions, Inc. evolves into a new company, Differencia.

See how the leaders in these stories learned from their mistakes and brought on new challenges. Decide how you would face these challenges if you were in the driver's seat in all or any one or more of the characters.

Dr. Cuomo and I have started authoring this trilogy because we believe in storytelling as the best way to identify with the human side of leadership. Dr. Cuomo's teaching points are from the collective experience of both of us, of learning from the dozens of leaders we have encountered working with over the past several decades. We learned from our mistakes as we learned from our previous leaders, on what was effective and ineffective, what was ethical and unethical, what was situational or altruistic in decision making.

Additionally, every decision we make is an "economic opportunity cost decision" where we need to decide where our best options lie when we lead. There are always consequences to every decision we make. Also, many will be affected by those decisions.

John DiCicco

Partner, The Authentic Leader LLC

Bibliography

"Leadership is a Choice." John DiCicco and Kenneth E. Strong, Jr., 2017.

"The Organization Man," William H. Whyte, 2002.

"The Leadership Gene," John DiCicco, 2017.

"Nurturing Love Through the Silence: Living With Alzheimer's" John DiCicco, 2011.

"On Air: My 50 Year Love Affair with Radio," Jordan Rich, 2021.

"Dare to Own You." Liz Bruner, 2021.

"The Seven Habits of Highly Effective People," Jim Collins, 2001.

"How to Win Friends and Influence People," Dale Carnegie, 1998.

"Talking to Strangers," Malcolm Gladwell, 2019.

"Outliers," Malcolm Gladwell, 2019.

"David and Goliath," Malcolm Gladwell, 2006.

"The Splendid and the Vile," Eric Larson, 2022.

"Truman," David McCullough, 1993.

"The Gift of Forgiveness," Katherine Schwarzenegger, 2020.

"Team of Rivals," Doris Kearns Goodwin, 2006.

"It's All About the Guest," Steve DeFilippo, 2013.

"Good to Great," Jim Collins, 2001.

"The Autobiography of Eleanor Roosevelt," Eleanor Roosevelt, 2014.

"The One Minute Manager," Ken Blanchard, 2003.

"Shouting at Leaves," Jennifer Mumba, 2021.

"The Wisdom of Crowds," James Surowiecki, 2005.

"The Trophy Kids Grow Up," Ron Alsop, 2008.

"Maximizing Cash Flow - The Path to Prosperity," Bruce J. Share, 2021.

"Tuesdays with Morrie," Mitch Albom, 2017.

"Eleanor," David Michaelis, 2021.

"Faith Still Moves Mountains," Harris Faulkner, 2022

"A Farewell to Arms," Ernest Hemingway, 2014.

"The Autobiography of Benjamin Franklin," 1791.

"Profiles in Courage," John F. Kennedy, 2006.

"The Biography of Abraham Lincoln," University Press, 2022.

"I've Been Thinking," Maria Shriver, 2018.

"Grit, The Power of Passion ad Persuasion," Angela Duckworth, 2018.

"The Art of Living," Edward Sri, 2006.

"The Autobiography of Calvin Coolidge," 2021.

"Herbert Hoover," William Leuchtenberg, 2009.

"American Lion," Jon Meacham, 2009.

"The Love Stories of the Bible Speak," Shannon Bream, 2023.

"So Help Me God," Mike Pence, 2022.

"Here's the Deal: A Memoir," Kellyanne Conway, 2022.

"Battle for the American Mind," Pete Hegseth, 2022.

"The Power of Focus," Jack Canfield, 2012.

"The Road to Freedom," Harriet Tubman, 2005

"Taxes Have Consequences: An Income Tax History of the United States," Arthur Laffer, Brian Domitrovic, and Jeanne Cairns Sinquefield, 2022.